Art of
CIGARS

CIGAR AFICIONADO'S

Art of
CIGARS

Edited by Marvin R. Shanken

publisher of *Cigar Aficionado*

COURAGE
BOOKS
AN IMPRINT OF RUNNING PRESS
PHILADELPHIA · LONDON

M. Shanken Communications, Inc.
New York

Printed in China

9   8   7   6   5   4   3   2   1
Digit on the right indicates the number of this printing

Library of Congress Cataloging-in-Publication Number 98-70171

ISBN 0-7624-0392-6

For subscriptions to *Cigar Aficionado*, please call: (800) 992-2442
Or write:
M. Shanken Communications, Inc.
387 Park Avenue South
New York, New York 10016

Visit our website at: www.cigaraficionado.com

Cover and interior design by Maria Taffera Lewis
Cover photograph by Charles Masters
Back cover photographs by Jeff Harris; Gaston Pacheco (bottom right)
Typography: Perpetua and Bell Gothic

Published by Courage Books, an imprint of
Running Press Book Publishers
125 South Twenty-second Street
Philadelphia, Pennsylvania 19103-4399

Acknowledgments

I would like to thank the following people who contributed to the making of this book: At M. Shanken Communications, Inc., Michael Moaba, Gordon Mott, George Brightman, Ann Berkhausen, Amy Lyons, Tara Smith, Martin Leeds, and Ellen Diamant. At Running Press, Stuart "Buz" Teacher, David Borgenicht, Greg Jones, and Ken Newbaker.

Contents

10

51

119

76

Introduction

The last few years have witnessed truly explosive growth in the world's enjoyment of fine cigars.

When I launched *Cigar Aficionado* magazine in 1992, a relatively small number of smokers were connoisseurs of this highly rewarding pleasure—and small wonder, considering that cigar smokers were often treated as pariahs, banned from public spaces and sometimes even their own homes.

Now, all that has changed. Sales of premium, hand-rolled cigars have skyrocketed in the last few years—seemingly limited only by the world's available supply of fine cigar tobacco. Tobacconists have sprouted up everywhere, and new brands have flooded the market. Cigar dinners and other cigar events, a real rarity in the early 1990s, are now too numerous to count.

Paralleling this upsurge in cigar smoking is renewed interest in what you might call the "material culture" of cigars—the smoking paraphernalia, cigar store Indians, cigar box art, and specially designed cigar environments like cigar bars and smoking rooms. This book is an introduction to, and a celebration of, that culture.

We've gathered informative essays and lots of sumptuous photographs for you to luxuriate in. First, you'll get an overview of the item that demonstrates that you're a committed cigar smoker—the humidor. Humidors can be modest and practical in nature, but they can also be superb demonstrations of the cabinetmaker's art, and you'll see some of the finest recent examples. We've also included some older humidors and cigar cases of historical interest.

Next, you'll find a panorama of what some call "cigar jewelry": the cutters and lighters that, in addition to their usefulness, help the smoker make a personal style statement. Some are made of precious metals, inlaid with rare woods, or enameled in dazzling colors, so the jewelry comparison is an apt one. These implements have an interesting past, as well, so we've included two pieces focusing on antique cutters and lighters as collectibles.

The cigar boom has led to a resurgence of interest in ashtrays among prominent designers and manufacturers of luxury goods. Whether crystal, silver, brass, stone, lacquered wood or porcelain, ashtrays can help you extend your style statement to your home or office. You'll find many gorgeous examples here, along with an in-depth look at how Limoges porcelain ashtrays are made.

Then, we survey three different categories of cigar-related art. No doubt the most familiar is the cigar-store Indian. (The Indian is actually only one variety among the many types of colorful, wooden mercantile sculptures that once decked city streets and are now highly prized by collectors.) The late nineteenth century—the heyday of the cigar-store Indian— was also a high point for cigars in the graphic arts. Capitalizing on the recent invention of commercial color printing, cigar manufacturers commissioned posters, box labels, show cards, and trading cards that are attention-grabbers even today. And on a more contemporary note, we present a number of recent examples of Cigar Art—art objects created on, in, or using wooden cigar boxes—by artists both little-known and world-famous.

Finally, we look at two very special kinds of environments designed with the cigar smoker in mind. Many wealthy industrialists of the Gilded Age built palatial residences for themselves; they often included a richly appointed smoking room, or at minimum, a room dedicated to male pursuits. Some of these mansions are now open to the public as museums, and we'll take you on a tour. Or if you'd prefer to explore some trendy, hip, totally of-the-moment smoking venues, check out the section on that modern institution, the cigar bar.

The cigar smoker's world is both fascinating and fun. The objects and places you'll discover in this book will enhance the pleasure you take in this most agreeable of pastimes. We hope you'll learn a little something here, but we also hope you'll kick back, settle in, and indulge your fantasies. Enjoy!

Marvin R. Shanken
Editor & Publisher
Cigar Aficionado

Travel humidors—like this one by Dunhill—while too big for local commuting are perfect for extended trips and vacations.

Chapter

Modern-Day Treasure Chests: Humidors and Cases

One

As the appreciation of cigars has grown, the diversity of sizes and styles of humidors and cigar cases has skyrocketed. As a general rule, those who smoke better cigars tend to have better humidors. The converse is also true: the finer the humidor, the better its contents. Having fine cigars and not having an appropriate humidor for them is like having a mint classic car and not keeping it in a garage. You are merely an acquirer, not an aficionado.

The demand for humidors and cases is driven not just by the growing number of cigar smokers, but also by the fact that many smokers are maintaining multiple humidors. Since the flavors of cigars mingle and intermarry in a humidor, some exacting smokers like to segregate special cigars into special humidors.

Today, there is an astounding range of cigar-protecting products offered—from the starkly functional to the astoundingly elegant, and from

Daniel Marshall's Treasure chest humidor
is hand-tooled in rare and precious
burl wood and lined with sweet
Spanish cedar.

From Savinelli's Rosewood Weave series, this unique humidor was created by cutting squares of rosewood and inlaying each piece by hand.

antique to high-tech—to meet the growing demand. Like a bottle of fine wine, a fine cigar is a natural, organic product which should be stored under closely controlled conditions. To be more specific, cigars should be kept in the conditions similar to those in which the tobacco grew, fermented, and was rolled. This is best achieved within a humidor.

To protect its contents against potentially damaging changes in humidity and temperature, a humidor should maintain an internal humidity in the range of 70–72 percent and an internal temperature of about 68–70 degrees Fahrenheit. On top of that, a humidor must allow some air flow. Cigars will grow moldy in a totally sealed humidor.

Most humidors will achieve this narrow set of conditions as long as you cure them properly, keep them at a normal room temperature (away from direct sun and other heat sources), keep water in their humidifying devices, and open them on occasion. Temperature is closely related to humidity, and if you control humidity, temperature tends to stay within an acceptable range.

A hygrometer, or humidity-measuring instrument, is not strictly necessary. Your finger, nose, and mouth are actually much finer gauges than hygrometers, particularly analog hygrometers. Whether or not a humidor has a thermometer and a hygrometer, the ultimate test remains the same: how are the cigars that have been stored in it? Many simple humidifiers pass this test. The fact that so many Americans have enjoyed fine Cuban cigars, despite the long-standing embargo, is, in large measure, a tribute to how well a traditional humidor can preserve a cigar. The stocks are getting low, but there are still genuine pre-embargo Cubans out there in perfect condition.

Some collectors with particularly large stockpiles are investing in more complex systems which actively control temperature as well as humidity. Some actually generate data logs of conditions, much like those seen near precious artwork in fine museums. These advanced systems are certainly justifiable when a large stock is stored in a building where the temperature is highly variable. For most cigar smokers, however, a less technical humidor will suffice, as long as it's a good humidor. To be good, humidors, like premium cigars, must be hand-made with the right materials, and put together in the right way.

For the wooden humidor, the proper interior wood is essential. Spanish cedar is the most traditional. It breathes and interacts with the cigars and the internal moisture. Most aficionados swear that cigars only get better when kept in a Spanish cedar lined humidor. There are a few other choices for the interior wood. Davidoff uses gaboon mahogany, an exotic wood that breathes like Spanish cedar, but has less odor. You can also find humidors lined with white cedar, red cedar, and rosewood. In almost every case, the interior wood is left unsealed so it can breathe. Michel Perrenoud, however, makes humidors with interiors of finished, sealed mahogany which have performed well in tests.

The requirements are equally strict for the wood layer

The King's Cupboard by Kreitman-Thelen is a high-quality cherrywood piece with a smooth finish and brass hinges; an electronic humidification system and built-in digital hygrometer insure quality control of the cigars.

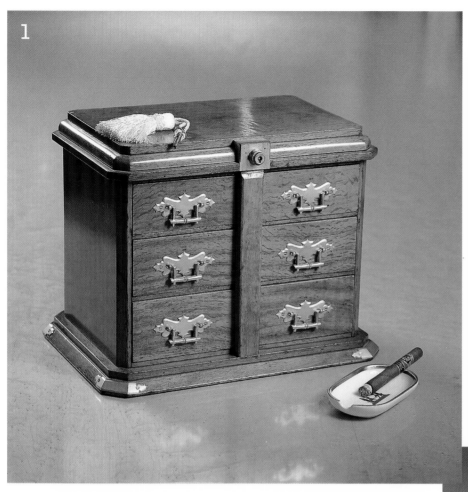

16

which makes up the structure of the humidor. The woods used must be carefully selected hardwoods. Mountain grown woods, which have grown more slowly and have a tighter grain, are best. This wood must be carefully kiln-dried; if it is not dried properly, it will warp and ruin the humidor.

Masterful carpentry is at least as important as the selection of woods. Most woodworking projects have a generous margin of error; wood bends and can be glued. Humidors, however, have to be crafted to tight tolerances. Excess glue will bleed out into the moist interior of a humidor, imparting an odor which can ruin cigars. And the lid must fit perfectly. In many cases, a humidor is constructed as a solid box, and the lid is then sawed off with a fine-toothed saw.

The outside layer of the humidor receives even more careful attention. The amount of artistry devoted to the exterior of some humidors rivals the treasure chests which once held royal jewels. Humidors have been covered in every imaginable wood, from burled walnut and bird's-eye maple to exotic selections such as African padauk, thuja, and macassar ebony. Thanks to their humidors, some cigar aficionados have become quite knowledgeable about exotic woods and the regions they come from. Often humidors made of exotic woods are finished simply, so the grain and color of the wood and the craftsmanship of the dovetail joints can be seen and appreciated. The finish may be simple, but it is rarely casual. The clear finish on an exotic wood humidor is often the product of nearly countless application, sanding, and tacking steps.

Few humidor exteriors are just straight lines and one single wood. There are often patterns created by contrasting inlays. Some humidors are among the finest examples of marquetry, an elegant form of wood collage. While many humidors are similar in size, they all have slightly different lines: a curve here, a different bevel angle at the joints, or different hardware. There are also sterling silver-, gold-, platinum-, and leather-encased humidors, as well as stone humidors.

Collectors look at older humidors not just as artifacts, but as useful items. The best humidors are those which have been in continuous use for years and have never warped or dried out. These are rare finds: why would anyone let one go? If a humidor has warped or split,

1. Antique solid elm, six-drawer cigar cabinet with Bramah lock, circa 1860. 2. Benson & Hedges mahogany humidor made for Douglas Fairbanks, 1919. 3. Victorian brass-mounted oak humidor in the form of a coach, late 19th century. 4. Burr walnut cigar cabinet with brass quadrants, brass inset side handles, and beveled glass doors, circa 1850. 5. Goldstone and Schilling vintage crocodile-skin cigar cases. 6. Diamond Crown three-finger robusto case.

it is generally not worth collecting. If, however, the humidor's only problem is that its humidifying device was clogged up and destroyed by the minerals in tap water, it's an easy matter to install a new humidifier; remember to use distilled water only. As with a new humidor, you must "season" a dried out humidor, slowly bringing it up to proper hydration.

Experienced collectors look for humidors which still have the key to

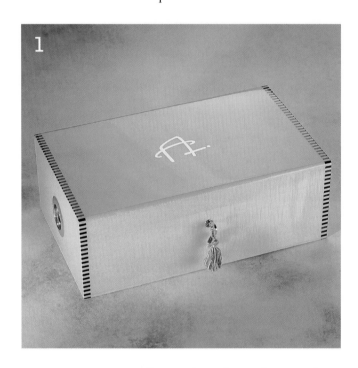

the lock. Locks on humidors are popular: they keep your cigars safe from the marauding hands of children, thoughtless visitors, and grabby relatives. Locks also help keep a humidor closed. Locks can be removed and changed but, to a collector, this can detract from the character and integrity of the antique.

Certain humidor makers produce special limited editions and number the individual humidors in the same way artists number prints, giving them immediate collectable status. Humidors which were once owned by famous smokers, or which were made to commemorate special occasions, can also take on extraordinary added value. The engraved plaques on larger humidors often give hints as to their provenance.

Today, humidors are being crafted in a host of shapes and sizes besides the wooden table or desk-top humidor, which is still the most common type. One can buy everything from a retrofitted military ammunition case to a custom built, fully conditioned room. There are vertical, glass humidors which look like old-fashioned cigar jars but have humidification systems built into their bases. There are also glass-walled cigar chests the size of night stands or retail display counters.

The greatest recent advances that are being made involve smaller humidors and cases. Not long ago, a cigar was at risk from the moment it was withdrawn from its home humidor. If even a short while passed before the cigar was smoked, it could get bashed, bruised, or simply dried out. Now there is a full range of smaller humidors and protective cases to insure complete protection.

Elegant small humidors can preserve a small supply of cigars for days. These "travel humidors" often include extra straps or blocks to keep cigars from shifting as you run for a flight. There are small, elegant models designed to be slipped into a briefcase, as well as larger models, including one that looks like a photographer's padded lens case. As with larger humidors, the quality of the construction and the presence of a well-maintained humidification device are crucial.

1. Elie Bleu offers many vivid designs like this one from the *Cigar Aficionado* collection. 2. Burr walnut Gothic-style three-drawer cigar cabinet, circa 1850. 3. Elie Bleu Vista Series humidor offset with the French designer's unique marquetry. 4. Walnut humidor presented to John F. Kennedy by Milton Berle in 1961. 5. Victorian macassar ebony smoker's cabinet, mid-19th century.

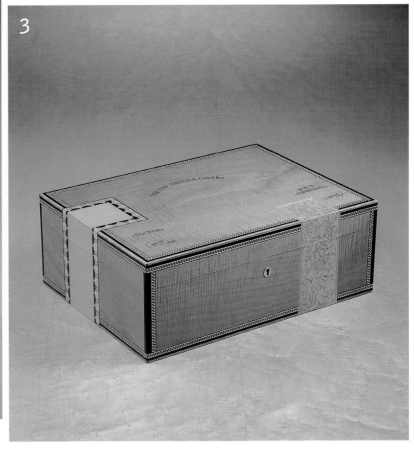

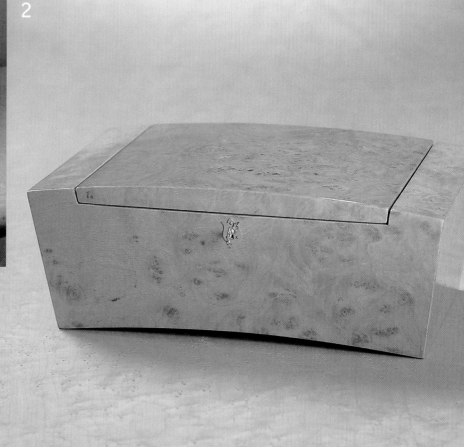

Cigar cases are even smaller than travel humidors, and few of them include humidification devices. Their function is to protect the cigar from being crushed or bent. Extremely functional cigar cases are made from high-impact plastic, but most aficionados prefer the graciousness of a leather case.

Leather cigar cases come in every size that cigars come in. Some have open compartments that can hold several cigars; others have fingers—distinct slots that hold a cigar in place even if you are only carrying one. Better cases are lined so there are no rough leather nubs which could tear a cigar. While cases are available in every color and thickness of leather, serious smokers avoid the ones made of wafer-thin leather that offer only minimal protection. An important test of a leather cigar case is the "sniff test." If the case emits a pungent smell of tanning chemicals or leather glue, you don't want it. That noxious smell would contaminate a good cigar in short order.

The next step down in size is the cigar tube, which is generally designed to hold a single cigar. (There are some double tubes sold, as well.) These tubes, made of glass or metal, protect a cigar and help keep it moist longer. Some tubes even include humidification devices. There are also a number of tubes and other cases designed to extinguish and hold partially smoked cigars. These are not for everyone. The common wisdom is that relighting a cigar after its been out for more than a few minutes is not worth it:

the cigar can taste bitter. Some smokers, however, just can't bear to toss out half of an 18 dollar cigar, so they like these gizmos.

Cigar tubes are like flasks. They don't hold much, but they are perfect when you want to carry along something special to cap off a special evening. Like flasks, cigar tubes are made in precious metals as well as base metals and are often stunningly etched. Recognizing this kinship, Nat Sherman sells a pewter "Stadium Flask" with room for the liquor of your choice, plus two cigars.

As cigar smokers become more serious about their pleasure, they become more careful about how they maintain their stocks. One dedicated cigar collector and smoker is described by his wife as a "cigar gardener." He maintains boxes of his favorite cigars in several different humidors, regularly checking the humidors and patiently rotating the collection on occasion. This endeavor takes up enormous amounts of time and has required a massive investment over the years. He insists, however, that he simply smokes the cigars for quality-checking purposes. He doesn't think of the cigars or the humidors as his property. They are his legacy to the grandchildren whose names the humidors bear.

1. Late-Victorian painted oak and inlaid mosaic commemorative humidor cabinet, late-19th century. 2. Commemorative walnut and cedar humidor issued by Cubatabaco celebrating the Fifth Centennial of the Discovery of Tobacco, 1994. 3. Fine carved walnut cigar cabinet presented to Winston S. Churchill from the Democracy of Cuba, October, 1941. 4. Davidoff's Macassar humidor made by hand in Switzerland from rare macassar wood.

Cutters, while all performing the same basic function, come in various designs and styles. Scissors and piercers shown here are made by, clockwise from top right: Colibri, Dunhill, Eloi, Cigar Savor, Avo Uvezian, and Davidoff.

Chapter

Making the Cut: Precision Cigar Cutters

Two

It's best to separate cigar cutters into two classes: old cutters, which can be great curios, souvenirs, and valuable collectibles, and new cutters, which are specialized precision tools. There are, of course, some old cutters which work almost as well as today's cutters, but, for the most part, as our standards of cigar cutting have risen, our cigar cutting technology has also improved.

Like nutcrackers, cork pullers, and door keys, the cigar cutter was made in all sorts of novelty forms—everything from dogs that cut the cigar when you moved their tails to women who nipped the cigar when you moved their limbs. The blades in these amusements were often poorly made, so using one often resulted in a torn cigar wrapper leaf. Similarly, there were many cheap cigar cutters made as promotional items for political candidates, retail stores, and travel destinations. These often had loose mechanisms and dull cutting edges, so they did not deliver precision cuts.

Wooden wedge cutters by the
Boston Cigar Co.

There are several ways to cut a cigar; it's a matter of individual taste. The various cutters shown here include, clockwise from top left: Cigar Savor piercer, T.T. Communications for Playboy guillotine, Cigar Savor piercer, Paul Garmirian guillotine, Avo Uvezian piercer, and a Boston Cigar Co. wedge.

These ineffective cutting tools were tolerated, in part, because less care was taken with the whole cigar storage and smoking process. An estimated three-quarters of the adult male population once smoked cigars, but the masses generally were not smoking carefully humidified premium cigars. There were a lot of lesser cigars which didn't merit the attention of a fine instrument.

In fact, many smokers used no instrument at all. They just moistened the cigar's end and used their fingernails to pinch an opening: a messy procedure, at best, especially given a dry cigar. Many bit the end off their cigar and spat it out. This was a less than precise procedure. It's hard to make an exact cut when you can't see what you are doing.

Many of those smokers who did use an instrument to open their cigars used a multipurpose instrument: their penknife. While a true gent kept his penknife sharp, he used it through the day for a variety of tasks. The blade which cut the cigar wrapper leaf was likely to have been sharpened with whetting oil before it was used to point a pencil, pare an apple, clean a fingernail, cut a hunk off a block of soap, and perhaps even scrape a shoe or horse hoof. It was not necessarily odorless. In addition, it took a steady, practiced hand to make a good cut with a penknife, which offered no help in positioning the cigar.

Another popular tool was the lance, or piercer, which created a narrow hole in the end of the cigar. Some nabobs carried sheathed gold lances on their watch chains, but many smokers used splinters, knife blades, pencil points, knitting needles, toothpicks, or nails. Lancing was a colorful practice, but one which didn't do good cigars justice. It opened a cigar with little chance of leaf flaking off into the smoker's mouth, but it created a tunnel in the center of the cigar

which led to a hot draw, rather than an even burn of all the different leaves blended into the "bunch" of the cigar.

In short, cigar cutting used to be a relatively primitive business. Today, you can still find cheap, unworthy cigar cutters, but there is no reason to use one when you can choose from a broad range of accurate, dependable, and often elegant cigar cutters.

The most common kind of cigar cutter is the single-bladed guillotine. This simple design concept lends itself well to compact cutters. Dunhill manufactures a classic version of the circular guillotine. To use it, you lift the blade to reveal an empty center circle, place your cigar in the circle, and press the blade home. Another classic guillotine cutter is encased in briar. Eloi makes elegant wafer-thin square and rectangular single-blade guillotine cutters which fit easily in a suit coat pocket without ruining the garment's drape.

Davidoff offers Zino double-bladed guillotines in which blades come in from both sides, so the pressure is applied evenly and the wrapper leaf is never pushed against a non-cutting surface. The trick with all guillotine cutters, and in fact, all cutters, is to steady the cigar against a surface so it stays in position when the cut is made. A small cut on the very end of the cigar won't give you enough draw. A cut too far up the barrel of the cigar will allow it to unravel and shed tobacco into your mouth. Allowing the cigar to move while you are cutting is likely to tear the wrapper. A recent innovation from Savinelli could address this potential problem; the blade is shaped like a batwing—a double concave curve with a point in the middle which pierces the cigar and holds it in place.

The very smallness of many guillotine cutters can be a drawback. Some smokers have trouble keeping steady anything that small and light. A smoker who fumbles with a single-bladed guillotine may have more control with a double-bladed model that has a finger grip at each end.

A cigar cutter of any type is only as good as its blades are sharp. It is often hard to get at and sharpen the blades in a guillotine cutter. Some guillotines now have "self-sharpening" blades. Absolute purists don't like them, but they seem to work reasonably well. Other guillotines have replaceable blades.

In addition to sharpness, general cleanliness is a concern. Close tolerances are a hallmark of guillotine mechanisms, and stray bits of tobacco can gum them up.

Inexpensive guillotine cutters, often with bodies made of colorful synthetic resins on which a logo and/or date has been imprinted, are becoming a popular promotional giveaway at events such as cigar dinners and the openings of cigar clubs. There is already a strong demand for these items, and they have every chance of becoming an extremely active area for collectors.

More expensive, engraved guillotine cutters are also becoming a popular business gift and gift for groomsmen at weddings. We have even heard of an ecstatic late-in-life father who passed a few out with cigars when his son was born.

Because guillotine cutters tend to be small, they are easily misplaced or purloined. One strategy to counteract this is to have your initials engraved into the cutter. Another is to buy a cutter with a ring that lets you attach it to a chain.

Cigar scissors are less portable than the guillotines, but in the hands of a practiced pro, they can deliver more reliable results. The best cigar scissors are made with the same steel, and the same techniques, as the finest surgical instruments. Manufacturers often claim that the hand-forged edges of these scissors are so strong they will stay sharp virtually forever.

Cigar scissors are sometimes plated in gold or decorated in some other fashion, but the beauty of these instruments lies in their precision function and versatility. A well-balanced pair of cigar scissors can cut a cigar of virtually any ring gauge. The issue of balance is more subjective than absolute: different scissors work better in different hands.

A quality pair of cigar scissors is something that you will want to keep handy. Some humidors are designed with magnets that allow scissors to be stored on the underside of the lid. Some smokers prefer to attach their cigar scissors to their humidor's hardware with a simple chain.

There are also devices which deliver different shapes of cut. Bull's-eye cutters, for example, cut a shallow hole into the end of the cigar with a twisting, not a shearing, action. These cutters look a bit primitive—like the backside of a bullet hole—but they are carefully machined and incredibly sharp. As with knives and scissors, it takes some practice to use a cutter of this type. You have to learn how to

Opposite page: Eloi produces a line of guillotine cutters that are not only beautiful but reliable. This page: The Churchill V by Colibri, which combines a cigar cutter and a lighter in one, comes in a variety of styles including, clockwise from middle: the silver hobnail, the gold diamond cut, and the silver satin finish.

The Zino Davidoff double-bladed

guillotine is the best cutter a

cigar smoker can buy.

align the cigar end with the blades, and you have to decide whether you prefer to rotate the cutter or the cigar. It's important, of course, that a bull's-eye cutter have the right aperture for the shape and ring gauge of the cigar you are cutting. If a bull's-eye cutter has blades of more than one diameter on it, they must be spaced so that the largest aperture has enough room around it for you to turn a thick cigar on it without hitting the neighboring blades.

The wedge cut, as its name implies, creates a wedge of open drawing surface, instead of a flat circular opening. Even though this cut is favored by some of the most respected tobacco stores, it remains controversial. Its proponents point out that it generally leads to a nicely drawing cigar. Its opponents say the wedge cuts too deeply into the center of the "bunch," and thus defeats careful construction by the cigar maker. (Incidentally, many of those old gents who used pocket knives to open cigars cut wedges into them.) In any event, the wedge cut is the wrong cut for a tense smoker with a strong jaw. If you chomp on the cigar, you'll collapse the wedge and stop the draw.

Many cigar stores have a large, nifty, counter-mounted machine which makes wedge cuts at the pull of a lever. This big machine is rarely found in private homes, but those private collectors and smokers who own one swear by them. Individuals are more likely to own a bar-shaped, portable wedge cutter in which the blades are on a spring-loaded mechanism that is pushed through a hole into which the cigar is inserted. Occasionally the cutting mechanism is mounted on a set of animal horns or some other colorful, collectible object.

While most smokers are satisfied with one cutter, some serious aficionados acquire wardrobes of cutters the same way they do a wardrobe of watches: a pair of scissors to use in the study at home when wearing the everyday watch; a resin-encased cutter to take to the duck blind or beach, where a water-resistant sports watch is just the ticket; and a refined, gold-plated or sterling silver cutter designed to complement elegant evening wear, as does a fine Lassale watch.

There is an undeniable pleasure to owning an old cigar cutter or two: they are fascinating and fun pieces of cigar ephemera. There is even greater pleasure in owning a piece of precision equipment which you can use to cut a perfectly made and stored premium cigar in preparation for a great smoke. Fortunately these pleasures are not, of course, mutually exclusive.

A pelican in brass with copper stand, engine room telegraph in brass, dachshund and shop wheel made of copper, all from the turn of the century.

Chapter

Grand Openings: Antique Cigar Cutters

Three

Cutters made from deer and elk antlers and horns, from early 1900s.

They dangled from watch-chains that stretched across the ample vests of prosperous gentlemen in the late nineteenth and early twentieth centuries. They snuggled in the pockets of average Joes. They promoted products as diverse as tobacco and sparkling water, or extolled the sights from Washington, D.C., to St. Paul, Minnesota. They came in such shapes as ballerinas, willowy Art Nouveau damsels, dachshunds and collies, pistols, shoes, Champagne bottles, a sailing ship's wheel, a medieval helmet, and a pot-bellied pig. They sat beside the cash registers in cigar stores. Today, they remain mute yet artful reminders of a bygone age. And they all had one elegantly simple, utilitarian purpose in common: to cut the head of a cigar cleanly for an expectant smoker.

Cigar cutters, made of precious metals, steel, iron, tin, or wood, once were the ubiquitous accessory of every smoker or tobacconist in an era when 70 to 90 percent of adult males puffed on cigars. Yet, like the purloined letter

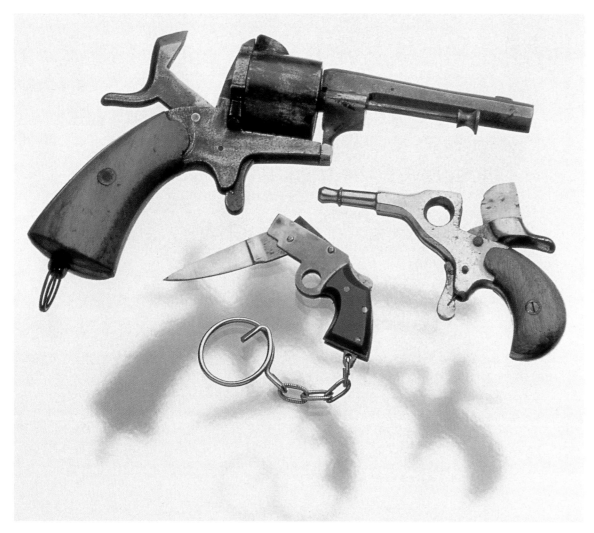

Above, clockwise from top: two gun cutters made of wood and iron, each about 100 years old, and a smaller gun with a plastic handle, circa 1930. Below: Antique cutters were designed with several functions in mid. These turn-of-the-century silver match safes held matches at the top and cutting implements at the bottom.

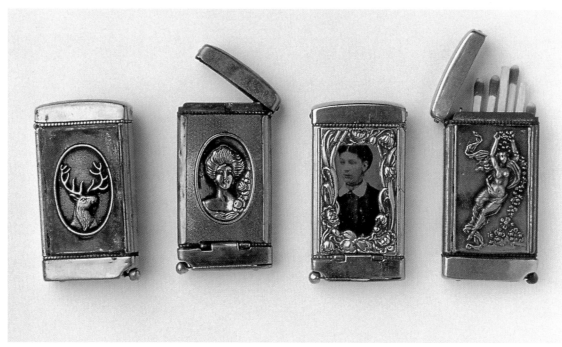

in Edgar Allan Poe's classic tale, they largely were hidden out in the open, often unseen in plain view. In the vast literature on cigars and smoking, little has been written about them. They have their devotees—collectors with canny eyes capable of seeing that a seemingly innocuous trinket or statuette really was made to clip cigars—but few scholars have concentrated on their origin and history.

Benjamin Rapaport, a world-class accumulator of smoking memorabilia and an acquaintance of collectors all over the globe, says that until recently he didn't know of anyone who had done serious scholarly work on cigar cutters. Rapaport calls cigar cutters "an elusive collectible" and the study of them "a very amorphous area of expertise." He has assembled the largest private collection of tobacco and smoking-related literature in the United States—and all he has ever seen has been "a few lines" about cutters in assorted tracts on cigars and smoking.

Yet the realm of antique cigar cutters may now become a whole new world for collectors to explore, given the phenomenon of cigars today. Some trailblazers have already forged a path into this unexplored region.

One such collector is Howard J. Thomas, 69, a semi-retired attorney in Silver Spring, Maryland, whose treasure trove of some 600 cigar cutters—many over a century old—is one of the largest ever assembled. "It just amazes me that there is so little information about cigar cutters," says Thomas, who for some 30 years has been scouring flea markets and antique stores for cutters and other cigar memorabilia.

When visiting a flea market, antiques store, or fair, Thomas says he looks "in almost every stall, but the smaller [stalls] generally have a small box with a glass top. [Cutters] usually are in there because the pocket ones were so small. They come in so many unusual shapes and forms that many a time you may see one and not know that it was a cigar cutter. The trick is in seeing and recognizing what you've got."

To identify a cutter, says Thomas, "first look to see if there's a round opening somewhere" in the little trinket—an aperture into which the head of a cigar could be inserted. "Then look to see if it has something that could cut the tip of a cigar," such as a tiny blade, or a pin for puncturing.

"You have to use your imagination to see if what you're looking at is a cutter," he continues. "Sometimes the people selling them don't even know what they've got. It's always wise to inquire of the dealers after you've looked at everything as to whether they've got any cigar cutters. Some dealers will say, 'Oh, yes,' and show you something you didn't spot."

Cigar cutters come in three basic varieties: pocket-size punchers or slicers; scissor-style clippers; and large "countertop" or combination-set models. The countertops most often are used in cigar stores; the combination sets are home accessories. Some of the cutters are whimsical; some scatological; some erotic. Few of the small ones bear any manufacturer's name or identifying date. Some are made of gold or silver; others are made of bronze; many more are made of common metals such as steel, iron, or tin. Collectors are known to have paid anywhere from a few dollars to several thousand dollars for antique cutters.

Collector Thomas has a copy of an advertisement sent to him some years ago by a friend, showing a bronze tabletop cigar cutter that features an Art Nouveau sculpture of a seminude woman reclining on a gray-and-black marble slab, her legs parted provocatively. The cutter is signed by "C. Kauba," identified in the undated ad as an American sculptor who lived from 1865 to 1922. The asking price for this gem was $2,500.

Thomas keeps most of his cutters in an antique cabinet in which a tailor or dressmaker once stored spools of thread. From its neat rows he can produce an astonishing and absorbing variety of cutters, including the figure of a little girl on a chamberpot, a can-can dancer and a tiny tennis player—all of which feature movable parts that can effectively cut the small, tapered tip of the kind of cigar most popular in the late 1800s and early 1900s. A sinuous Art Nouveau lady is stamped with the date "2-2-95" (surely that isn't 1995); a bottle opener that doubles as a cutter promotes "Virginia Natural Water Carbonated Ginger Ale" and is dated "10-12-09."

Thomas also has a wide variety of tabletop cutters, which he keeps on the shelves and bookcases around his home. Some of the cutters were used as advertising accessories, especially for cigar makers and merchants, and some were part of elegant companion sets that also featured a cigar container, matches, and an ashtray. These were the sort of accouterments a prosperous individual would have had sitting beside his brandy or Port nearly a century ago.

A mong Thomas' advertising novelty items is a dachshund whose tail can be lifted and lowered to slice the end of a cigar. The cutter proclaims that "Paraflint Chatfield's Permanent Roofing Lasts Longer." Stallman and Son of York, Pennsylvania, makers of "Clark, the Popular 5-cent Cigar," and Grammers and Ullrich Reliable Cigars in Chicago had their names embossed on large, spring-loaded tabletop models. After being wound, these cutters, with a wicked chop, would automatically clip the tip of an inserted cigar.

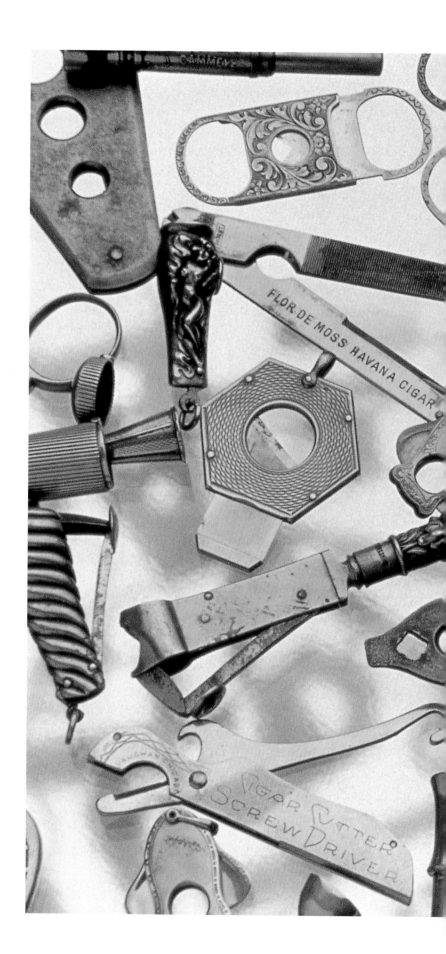

Cutters come in a variety of styles: some are designed in the guillotine fashion, while others use a scissors or some other mechanism. These models are made of brass and silver, circa 1920s.

These point-of-purchase, advertising-embossed cutters often featured a small kerosene lamp. Cigar store patrons could clip their cigar, put a proffered wick in the lamp's flame, light up their smoke and go on their way. The second volume of the Antique Advertising Encyclopedia, published in 1985 by veteran dealer Ray Klug, featured eight pages of photographs depicting such cutters. A guide in the back of the book gave suggested prices ranging from $200 to $3,500.

Human teeth, most likely the oldest form of cigar cutter, are still deemed *de rigueur* by some and *dèclassè* by others. In Alfred H. Dunhill's elegant little 1954 volume, *The Gentle Art of Smoking,* he observed without comment: "In the United States it is customary to bite off the end of green (or fresh) cigars."

In *The Connoisseur's Book of the Cigar*, Zino Davidoff noted that while American smokers "in general, use a cutter," others—"not the most sophisticated," he sniffed—"chew off the end." This procedure, Davidoff wrote, "does not permit much precision. I realize that some smokers are past masters of this technique, but I never practice or recommend such a method."

Curiously, Dunhill and Davidoff unwittingly disparage the means by which the greatest cigar smoker of the twentieth century—Winston Churchill—prepared his cigars for lighting: a quick thrust with a piercer. As William Manchester described in the first volume of his biography of Churchill, Sir Winston liked to wet the end of his cigar and puncture it with a long wooden match. Then he would blow through the cigar from the other end to ensure that it would draw.

Evidently unaware of (or in dispute with) Churchill's habits, Dunhill warned that while piercing a cigar head exposes the minimum amount of filler and thus helps the wrapper to keep tobacco tar away from the tongue, "the smoke and moisture concentrate in one narrow passage and may result in a bad draw." He also considered it "unwise to blow through a cigar in order to remove particles of broken leaf, because this injects moisture from the breath."

To Davidoff's mind, a lance would "savagely pierce the delicate head of the cigar, thereby creating a useless funnel for an excess of heat, tar-filled smoke, and a bitter taste." Davidoff also was adamant on another point: "Cigar cutters are fine, but not the penknife."

Many of the antique cutters in Howard Thomas' collection not only are tiny enough to fit in a vest or pants pocket without causing a bulge, but the holes they have for the cigar head are small as well. David Wright, curator of the Museum of Tobacco Art and History, says that nineteenth century cigars "were mostly tapered, and that's the reason the [cutters were] small. The cigars [themselves] were smaller. This idea of having a big cigar is more of a twentieth century phenomenon."

Wright notes that the museum (funded by the United States Tobacco Manufacturing Co., the parent company of United States Tobacco International), is the only repository of its kind in North America. Of the nearly 1,500 tobacco-related items in the museum's private collection—of which some 1,000 are on display—only six are cigar cutters. Among them are an impressive figure of a reclining lion—a beautiful piece, about six inches in length, made of brass—a small, gold "finger guillotine," and a miniature shoe that holds matches in its toe and contains a cutter in its heel.

"It's interesting to see the different variations and styles," Wright says. "When you get into tabletop variations, where you have a whole piece devoted to not just the cutter but [also] a cigar holder, match holder, and ashtray, that's a nice statement, because the themes of most of these companion sets are just typical slices of Victorian life.

And a lot of them tend to be humorous themes. It's really fun."

Wright's advice for would-be collectors: "Go for variety. Look for condition. Any damage to the piece detracts from its future appreciation value. If it is gold, see that the gold is not worn down to the base metal. If it is tin, look to see that it has not been repaired. If it is wood, look to see that no part is broken.

"Make sure all the parts [of the cutter] are in place; that nothing's missing. If it has been painted, you want the paint to be in fine condition. If it has been repaired, pass it up. If it is metal and has been dropped, dented, or banged around, you don't want it. It should be in fine working order."

With the arrival of machine-made cigars that were pre-perforated for the customer's convenience, cigar cutters became essential only for connoisseurs of the finer, handmade cigars. Baltimore, once home to nearly 60 cigar factories and dozens of tobacconists, had manufacturers and purveyors of both. At the city's century-old cigar store, Fader's, third-generation owner Ira B. "Bill" Fader Jr. has a few cigar cutter artifacts from the days when his grandfather Abraham had 80 employees hand-rolling cigars.

One is a cutter that sat by the cash register and could accommodate three different-sized cigars. Insert a cigar in the appropriate hole, depress a lever, and the cigar is neatly clipped. The slogan this cutter sports is for the Fader-made Iraba, "the GOOD cigar." (The "Iraba" was named for Bill's father, Ira B. Sr.)

In *The Connoisseur's Book of the Cigar*, Zino Davidoff observed diplomatically that no single method of cutting a cigar is preferable to another. One can pinch the cigar head, and if "the fingernail is long and sharp enough, a simple slit . . . can be made in the wrapper," he

wrote. He advised that the "cut made with the nail should not be too wide or too deep," and suggested wetting the end of the cigar if it is a little dry in order to facilitate this method.

Coming to the apparently necessary defense of those whose use of a cigar cutter was considered effete, Davidoff wrote: "Despite the opinion of some, it is not shameful to use such an instrument, especially if it has been well-chosen. Ordinary cigar cutters, which make a round or beveled cut, are not to be condemned."

Sometimes, Davidoff warned, "you must watch that the cut is not made too deeply. Do not forget that the beveled cut produces more drawing surface than the superficial circle opening." Regardless of method, he wrote, the key was that the "opening should be small, reasonable, in proportion to the cigar, and made so that an appropriate amount of smoke will be produced. The opening ought to be clean."

Alfred Dunhill advised in *The Gentle Art of Smoking* that while there are many ways of piercing a cigar, much "depends on the condition of the cigar." He noted: "When handling mature cigars, some smokers crack open the end by squeezing it between the finger and thumb, but unless the cigar is in excellent condition and the butt perfectly made, this can be disastrous.

"Perhaps the most satisfactory method," Dunhill wrote, "is a clean-shaped cut made by a cigar cutter, because this ensures the removal of broken leaf and provides a passage for the smoke that does not concentrate all of it upon a small area of the tongue." He suggested that tapered cigars with a pointed head should be cut "with a straight cutter or turned against the blade of a sharp knife and cut straight across."

The point, as Count Mippipopolous told Hemingway's hero Jake Barnes in *The Sun Also Rises*, is that after all is said, done, and clipped, the cigar should "really draw." —NEIL A. GRAUER

S.T. Dupont Maduro Collection lighters (table top version on right, pocket version on left).

Chapter

Matchless Accessories: Cigar Lighters

Four

A lighter gives you instant access and control of one of the most useful and terrifying forces in the universe: fire. For centuries, our ancestors lived in fear of fire. Once they leaned to control it, dwellings became more comfortable, food became better tasting, and the advent of night (with its encroaching predators) became less daunting. The ability to create fire at will was a cornerstone of civilization. Today, we have fire so well controlled that we rarely see it at work—in the engines of our cars, the ovens in our kitchens, and the furnaces in our basements. Yet the desire to be able to carry and create a flame remains deep within us. That's why Boy and Girl Scouts happily spend so much time using a magnifying glass to focus the sun's rays on dry tinder, and why it remains such a pleasure to have a trusty lighter at the ready.

While cigar smoking is a venerable pleasure with long traditions, cigar lighters and cigar lighting have changed dramatically over the last

Sterling silver "Elite General"
lighter by Colibri.

45

Cigar lighters come in a wide range of designs and materials, so it is easy to find one that's an appropriate accessory for your sense of style.

generation. Quite a few of our fathers lit their first stogies with matches filched from the shelf above the stove, in the days before ranges had pilot lights. Many of their fathers lit their first cigars using a lamp which exuded the distinctive reek of kerosene. Today, these methods are frowned upon. Kerosene lamps have gone the way of steam locomotives, and most aficionados feel that the sulfur odor of a lit match detracts from the delicate taste and aroma of fine cigars. Most of today's smokers start their cigars using the clean, simple flame of a lighter.

There are, of course, different schools of thought concerning lighters. Some traditionalists carry a torch for the conventional fluid-filled lighter, particularly the all-American "Zippo." They love the fact that these lighters have been carried by countless soldiers in the field. They like the way the Zippo clicks closed with an audible snap. A few even remember how these were the first lighters that could stand up to a breeze at the beach. To these aficionados, the Zippo is a classic, like a Harley-Davidson motorcycle.

Others, however, feel that Zippos and their kin are as outmoded as the crank-started car that needs a special mixture of oil and gas at every fill-up. To begin with, these detractors are horrified by the idea of lighting a hand-rolled cigar with a fluid-based system. They detect an oily odor which they consider an assault on their palate. They prefer gas-burning lighters because the flame from butane gas is virtually odorless and tasteless. On top of that, they don't think all the fuss with fluids, funnels, and wicks is necessary.

The fluid fans counter with the durability of their lighters. There are plenty of forty-year-old Zippos around, and, given that they are guaranteed for life, they are likely to be around for a long time to come. Few butane lighters are likely to last that long before they clog

up. The fluid lighter folks also dismiss the "taste" concerns. They maintain that if you light your cigar properly—with the cigar held above, and not in, the flame—all of the fluid flavors will burn off and dissipate before you take the first draw. They have also heard a few stories about friends of friends whose gas-filled lighters exploded when lit or when carried in pressurized airplane cabins.

Partisans of gas-powered lighters are quick to point out that these lighters contain several characteristics which make them superior sources for cigar ignition. First and foremost, you taste the cigar, not the lighter. Also, with gas lighters, the nozzle can be designed, or a second nozzle can be added, to create flames of varying shapes.

Gas-powered lighters allow flames of adjustable heights, but this is of more concern to pipe smokers than it is to cigar aficionados. (Pipe lighting and cigar lighting are very different arts. For example, a flame that can be drawn downward is useful when lighting a pipe, but of little utility when lighting a cigar.) Cigars can be lit well from small heat sources, such as the small "after-burn" above heating elements in "flameless" lighters. A small flame is fine, but a weak, inconsistent flame is unacceptable. It tempts the smoker to shove the cigar all the way into the flame, when the proper technique is to toast your cigar just above the top of the flame. Putting a cigar into a flame can overheat it, and can lead to ash dropping onto a heating element, which will eventually burn out the coil.

It is the width of flame that matters most to cigar smokers, particularly those who smoke the larger ring-gauge sizes. A wide flame makes it easy to achieve an even light. You don't have to worry so much about rotating the cigar end through the flame. An uneven light can lead to a "runner," where one part of the cigar burns back faster than the rest.

There is, of course, no ultimate answer in the feud between gas and fluid lighters. Neither side is likely to convert members of the other, nor is there any agreement about the other style's benefits. The ultimate judges of lighters are the smokers who use them, and they use highly personal criteria. Some like the ease of use that a long flint rollbar on the side gives a lighter, while others like the sturdy resistance of a top-mounted cog wheel. Some like the classic mechanical intricacy, while others prefer the sleek modern look of a barely-visible heating element sparked by piezo-quartz.

Lighters are as much a matter of style as they are of function. If a cigar smoker simply wants an odorless gas lighter with a wide, cigar-friendly flame, there are utilitarian lighters which look a bit like plastic flame throwers that do the trick quite nicely. Most fine cigar smokers, however, seem to prefer carrying a more refined accessory, and most gift givers like to bestow classier-looking mementos. Like the car you drive, the pen you write with, and the watch you wear, a lighter can communicate volumes about your sense of self and sense of style.

This helps explain why the classic rectangular "tank" shape has been interpreted in so many ways. The dimensions vary from a chunky block, comfortable in even the hammiest hand, to a slim rectangle which nestles nicely in smaller hands. Logos, slogans, and ads of all kinds have been painted and glued onto the lower-end models, creating a massive class of collectibles.

The broad planes of the front and back of the rectangular lighter also lend themselves perfectly to engraving. Look at your friends'

lighters and you are likely to discover what means the most to them. You may discover their nicknames, real birth dates, favorite sayings, names of children or, if they are forgetful, home phone numbers engraved in a utilitarian, durable metal, such as nickel-plated brass, or a more expensive metal or plating such as pewter or sterling silver.

Unengraved models often sport exotic exterior surfaces. Patterns of all sorts have been engraved into the metals of fine cigar lighters. Every imaginable wood veneer has been applied, from sturdy American walnut to rare African woods. Lighters have even been encrusted with coins or gems.

For the most part, the most highly-prized—and most expensive—lighters are those with intricate inlay or enamel work. These lighters have often been sold in jewelry stores, and rightfully so. They are less tools than they are portable artworks. The enameled side of a lighter can be a simple, rich, surprising color (such as a deep, vibrant blue), or a combination of colors arrayed in abstract patterns.

The range of lighter shapes also goes far beyond the classic rectangle. Some lighters are shaped like a tube of lipstick. Others curve the rectangle's corners in eccentric ways. They can be round, oval, or any other shape so long as there are no sharp edges which could gouge hands or pockets.

Many lighters have additional features built into them. Some are as simple as a ring so the lighter can be kept on a chain, or a clip to hold it in your pocket. (Some brave souls use these clips as money clips, but most prefer to keep their folding cash farther away from flames.) Others have more complex added features, including cigar cutters and golf ball markers. One well-known tour-de-force is the lighter with an elegant clock in its side.

Some lighters, particularly those with a fine veneer, inlay, or enam-

Photo top right, clockwise from bottom left: Dunhill, Zippo, Zippo, S.T. Dupont, S.T. Dupont, IM Corona, and Prometheus. Photo bottom left, clockwise from top left: Davidoff, S.T. Dupont, S.T. Dupont, Zippo, Dunhill, and IM Corona for Savinelli. Photo bottom right: Prometheus "Solar" lighter (shown with a Peronneau cigar ashtray).

el finish, come with cloth or leather cases. These cases tend to be as beautiful as the lighters themselves. The leather is usually buttery-soft and flawlessly finished.

It is likely that there will be a proliferation of innovative lighter designs in the coming years. We will see novelties which are the equivalent of the once ubiquitous gag item: the lighter in the shape of a pistol.

There may also be renewed interest in large lighters. For some, the complete office once had an enormous marble lighter perched near the marble ashtray. It's also likely that someone will develop a large lighter for the staff at cigar clubs and cigar bars—the incendiary brother of the four-foot tall pepper mill.

These large lighters may appeal to pyromaniacs, but they are unlikely to catch on with true aficionados. Lighting a fine cigar will remain an intimate, personal act, and aficionados will use a small lighter for the same reason that a diamond cutter uses small tools. The small size allows you to comfortably control the act of lighting your cigar. It challenges your skill and, with every perfectly lit cigar, provides a small sense of accomplishment and pride.

Even the humblest lighters have a way of becoming heirlooms. Many of the fans of fluid lighters inherited a lighter from a grandfather or favorite uncle. Because lighters are used so often, they become intimately associated with their user. The smell of a fluid lighter can be as evocative as the smell of a cigar, a tweed, a leather, or a shoe polish. We get a sniff and we remember in vivid detail a long lost mentor or family member.

One sales manager we've met treasures his lighter. Not because it's expensive or beautiful, but because it belonged to his first boss. As the boss aged, he would make it a point to hold the lighter in his hand through every meeting. Whenever he started to doze off, he would feel the lighter slip, or hear it clatter to the table, and wake up to business again. The manager gives all new salespeople a lighter, whether they smoke or not, to let them know that he expects them to lose some sleep, but won't tolerate them sleeping on the job.

Because fluid lighters are so durable, it is almost impossible to throw them out. They are held onto. Broken ones are stashed in sock drawers or workbench shelves, along with loose springs and flints, for later examination and tinkering. Even spouses and children who hate smoking often have trouble tossing a loved-one's lighter.

Gas-powered lighters may not have the same memorable aroma or reassuring hinge click as fluid models, but what makes a lighter an heirloom is not its fuel. What makes a lighter special is its superior design, elegance, and the recollections it evokes.

Many of today's lighter models are destined to become collectible classics or coveted inheritances. There are Dunhills and S.T. DuPonts, for example, which are timeless and will be in style in two years and in twenty. Even if they did not know the original owner, people years from now will look at them and realize that they did a great job of lighting a cigar, in remarkable style.

S.T. Dupont Limited Edition lighter.

ZIMMER SPLINT COMPANY

B.P.O.E.

CARBORUNDUM
TRADE MARK

U.S.S. FULTON
AS-11

Antique Zippo lighters are a favorite
among collectors.

Chapter

Old Flames: Collectible Lighters

Five

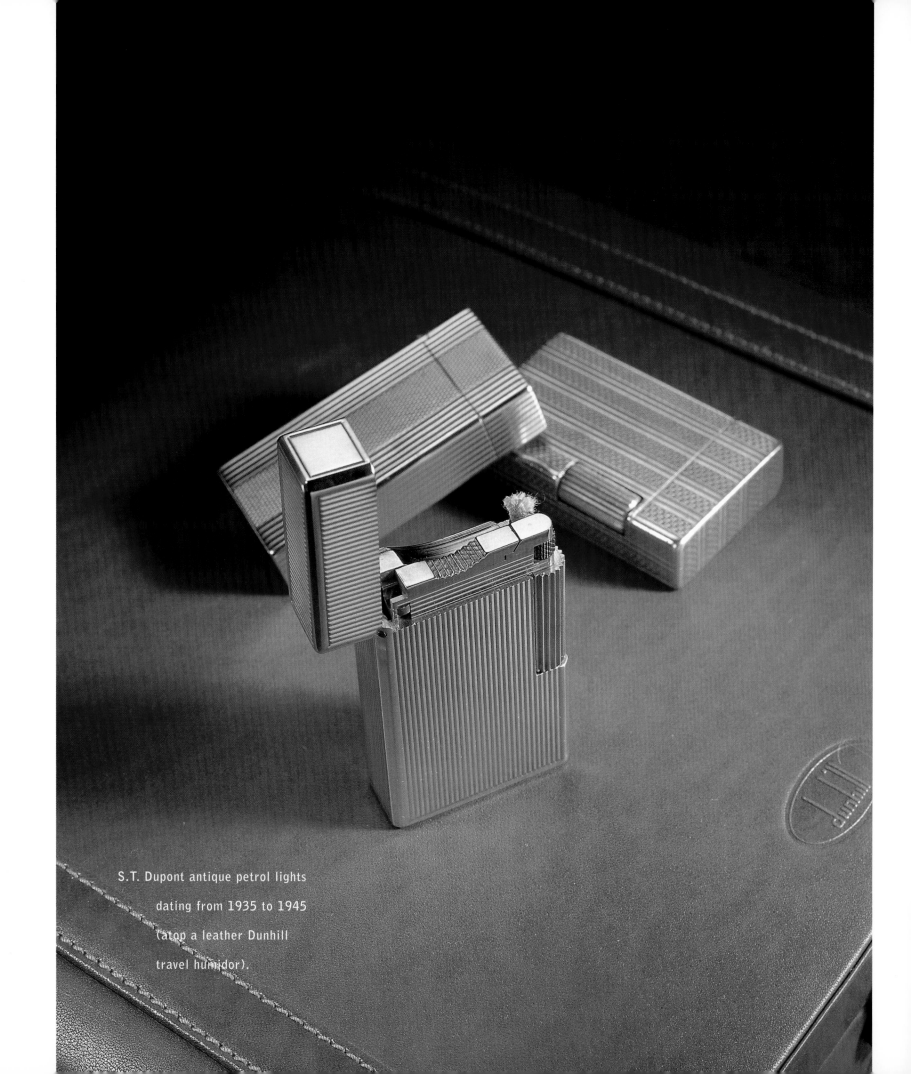

S.T. Dupont antique petrol lights

dating from 1935 to 1945

(atop a leather Dunhill

travel humidor).

54

It can stop a bullet, clip a cigar, tell you the time, sign a check and, by the way, light a Cohiba. "It," of course, is the cigar lighter.

Lighters double as walking sticks, pens, clocks, tape measures, flasks, compasses, and picture frames. "The most unusual ones are those you look at and say, 'This couldn't possibly be a lighter!'" says Richard Weinstein, a New York dealer and lighter-repair expert of 20 years.

"A lighter is the epitome of a great idea, designed brilliantly and executed with the highest level of precision engineering," says Richard Ball, a London-based dealer and the founder of the 220-member nonprofit Lighter Club of Great Britain.

Lighter designs are often based on the shapes of airplanes, cameras, cars and pistols, or they feature celebrities and icons. Charlie Chaplin, FDR, Popeye, and the Statue of Liberty are but a few of the characters gracing the cases of some of these portfires.

The earliest lighters were tinder pistols, invented in the mid-seventeenth century shortly after the first flintlock firearms were made. Resourceful gunsmiths began recycling broken pistols, using the barrel to store tinder rather than gunpowder. The trigger released a mechanism that struck a piece of iron and directed the sparks onto the tinder, which would ignite. Table tinder pistols were often combined with candlesticks, clocks, and inkwells, while pocket models were designed to be carried like a weapon.

cerium to create "Auer metal," which essentially became the small flint still used in lighters today. Welsbach's invention made lighters more efficient, safer, and ultimately more popular.

"Twentieth-century petrol lighters can be divided among the manual, semiautomatic, and automatic models," writes Dutch lighter expert Ad van Weert in his book *The Legend of the Lighter*. Manuals are striker lighters in which a flint is attached to part of the instrument. The body contains a steel rod enclosing a wick soaked in petrol. By

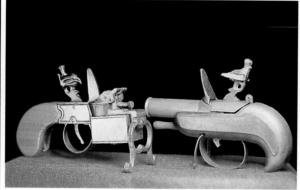

From the Ronson Lighter Collection (left to right): Evan's Enamels, 1950s; Dunhill tinder pistols—gun with barrel, circa 1930 and gun without barrel, 1950; Democrat vs. Republican, circa 1935

In 1823, German chemist Johann Wolfgang Döbereiner created a table lighter that used hydrogen gas to produce a flame. But Döbereiner's lamps, though convenient, were apt to explode. The solution arrived about 60 years later with the fusee, an early version of the wick lighter. A steel wheel struck a flint, producing sparks that ignited the fusee (a piece of cord submerged in fuel).

There is a certain irony in the fact that lighter collecting is a rather recent pursuit. Although fire is one of man's oldest discoveries, lighters as we know them are basically a twentieth-century invention. In 1903, Austrian chemist Carl Auer von Welsbach combined iron and

striking the steel rod on the flint, a series of sparks ignites the wick. On semiautomatic models, the cover automatically rises when the turnwheel is triggered (or, in some models, lifting the cover activates the flint wheel). In either case, the cover has to be closed manually to extinguish the flame. The automatic lighter requires the use of just one hand and one finger. Ronson Lighters founder Louis V. Aronson achieved this in 1926 with the Banjo model. His advertising slogan said it all: "Push, it's lit; release, it's out."

Soon thereafter, nearly everyone had a lighter—and large numbers of these early models have survived. Zippo, the most popular brand among collectors, has produced some 300 million lighters since the company's inception in 1932. Every Zippo is guaranteed for life; and they're all collectible. Many lighter buffs own more than a thousand. Ten-year veteran Larry Tolkin owns more than 2,000 lighters, including one of the world's most extensive Ronson collections. National Lighter Museum founder Ted Ballard's collection of 20,000 lighters was born in the 1930s with a gift from his grandfather.

"We're trailblazers," says Barry Hoffman, a Boston real-estate

10,000 collectors in the United States remain unaffiliated with either organization.

If perhaps less visible, lighter collectors are certainly not less passionate than other collectors. The Club Italia L'Accendino ("The Lighter") calls its highly regarded bimonthly newsletter "Lighters Mania." Its British counterpart is "Blaze." All of the clubs sponsor local swap meets and provide an invaluable networking venue. "It's always hot news when someone in the lighter community finds a

From the Ronson Lighter Collection (left to right): bronze dragon made in Germany in the 1950s; two bulldogs, late 1920s, early 1930s; "The Wonder Light"—a Rosie O'Neil Kewpie doll.

developer who's amassed more than 800 lighters in four years. "You can still find some very rare, highly collectible pieces at local flea markets. There are still a lot left to discover."

Lighter collecting has seen remarkable growth in the past five years. There are seven international lighter clubs, two of them based in the United States. The 800-member Texas-based On the Lighter Side (OTLS) holds its annual convention the second weekend of June in alternating cities, and the 250-strong Pocket Lighter Preservation Guild (PLPG) assembles each April in Chicago. Although club membership has grown in the past two years, some

piece that no one's ever seen before," says Tolkin. "And this happens every two or three months."

Both rarity and unusual mechanical design affect the value of a lighter. Rarity is a function of the number produced, and the number that have survived. It is not necessarily related to age; some rare pieces are not old. (They may have been custom-made or produced recently but in limited quantities.) Table lighters are rarer than pockets (and generally more valuable); approximately seven table models were produced for every thousand of the pocket variety.

Still, the market value of a lighter depends in part on its age. A specimen that is especially characteristic of a particular period, such as an Art Deco enamel, assumes a greater value. Another important consideration is the materials used to make a lighter; precious metals and enamels command higher prices. A built-in secondary function (such as a lighter that doubles as a pocket knife or humidor) makes a piece more precious; timepieces and jewels are further price boosters.

Makers are significant, with Dunhill and Cartier topping the list. Ronson (known in its early days as Art Metal Works) and Evans are the principal American brands, with Zippo in a category by itself. The Austrian IMCO, British Colibri, French DuPont and Van Cleef & Arpels, Swiss Thorens and La Nationale, and Italian Saffo are all highly regarded hallmarks. After World War II, many Japanese companies reproduced all sorts of gimcracks containing concealed lighters. Stamped "MIOJ" (Made in Occupied Japan) as required by law, lighter designs ranged from Wurlitzers to sewing machines to motor cars.

Alfred Dunhill Ltd. fancies its lighters the Rolls Royces of the trade. Alfred Dunhill, the London-based company's founder, established a dictum that stated, "It must be beautiful, it must be the best of its kind, and it must last." British royals, Winston Churchill, maharajas, and other foreign dignitaries are among the customers listed in shop registers past and present.

Two Dunhill lighters are even included in the *Guinness Book of World Records*. The world's longest lighter is Dunhill's Meter Rule, a late-1930s architectural piece in the form of a silver-plated box. The most expensive lighter fetched £37,500 (approximately $56,535) in 1986: A Dunhill model named the Lighthouse, it consisted of a two-foot-high, 18-karat gold beacon flickering atop a "rock island" crafted from a 112-pound amethyst.

In 1934, Dunhill created a single Dorothy Rose Basket lighter to spark interest in the company. It was a miniature platinum-and-gold basket containing a cluster of 60 rubies, cut in the shape of damask roses. Lifting the basket's handle exposed a lighter nestled inside. The basket has since disappeared and remains the object of an intense, but thus far futile, search.

Another highly sought Dunhill is a 1938 boar's tusk table lighter pictured in the company's catalogue for that year, thought to be a one-of-a-kind item or a very limited edition. No Tusk has been found to date, yet Dunhill collectors continue to look, convinced one may eventually turn up in India.

It is not known just how many of the Tusk and some other Dunhill models were produced, because World War II bombings of London destroyed many of Dunhill's records. What survived is stored in the company's London Archives Collection, including more than 1,200 lighters, advertisements, photographs, and catalogues.

Most lighters do remain on the shelf, unused by owners who hanker after only those in the best condition. Because condition generally influences the value of any collectible, a piece found in its original package, unopened, is worth about 30 to 50 percent more. The sturdier the stuff it's made of, the better its chances for surviving intact and in good condition; thus lighters made of fragile materials, like glass, are more valuable since they have a lower survival rate. The Massachusetts-based Evans Company made a series of lighters with fruit- and egg-shaped enameled cases that fit into this category. Hand-painted or enameled in the Fabergè style, these strawberries, apples, pears, pineapples, acorns, and eggs were made from 1948 to 1959.

Fame also counts. One New York collector owns lighters that

belonged to Ethel Barrymore and Jose Ferrer. Another collector has a lighter inscribed by Joseph Kennedy, given on Christmas 1927. Sotheby's auctioned Marlene Dietrich's Dunhill. Some devotees create whole collections around this motif.

Hollywood was a big market for lighters in the glamour-struck 1940s and 1950s. In 1947, there were 147 lighter manufacturers in Los Angeles alone. In Hitchcock's 1951 film *Strangers On a Train*, a Ronson Adonis lighter fills half the screen during its moment in the limelight. During the '50s and '60s, it was common practice for performers to give out lighters. They bore the signatures, and occasionally the images, of performers like Bob Hope, Dean Martin, and Jerry Lewis. (The late Frank Sinatra was a collector himself.)

Most hobbyists fine-tune their collections, with some themed around golf, naked women, commemorative events, electric lighters, specific brand names, nineteenth-century mercury-filament cap lighters, American corporate logos, or Zippo U.S. Navy lighters. Not surprisingly, Ugo Beretta, proprietor of the renowned Italian firearms company, has a collection that specializes in pistol lighters.

Guns and lighters are a frequent match. As fundamental gear for soldiers and sailors in both World Wars, lighters provided flames for illumination, rescue beacons, cooking and warmth, and of course,

Cartier oval gas lighter in yellow gold with a sunbeam design. Hammer and ends of burnished gold with a cabochon emerald, 1945.

lighting up. Due to frequent dampness, matches were often useless. This is one explanation for the proliferation of "trench art" lighters. These were makeshift models said to have been crafted during the trench warfare of World War I. Cartridge cases, bullets, helmets, coins, and other debris were used to create rudimentary mechanisms with highly inventive designs. Trench art is itself a category of collectibles.

During World War II, both Zippo and Ronson "went to war." Ronson contributed metal hinges used on a particular torpedo bomber, and Zippo sent lighters. The Zippo form has remained virtually unchanged (except for a quarter-inch height reduction) since it first appeared in 1932. The standard chrome cases were made memorable by soldiers who engraved words on to and attached badges and souvenirs to them, customizing their Zippos and providing tidbits of military history.

Perhaps the present lighter craze is due in part to the disappearance from our daily lives of an object that was once a personal effect—not unlike a wristwatch—reflective of one's identity. Urban Cummings, the Ronson expert with a collection 10,000 strong, speculates: "Wick lighters are something from the past that last. They represent a time, before disposables, when values were different."

—*NANCY WOLFSON*

Feuille de Tabac (Tobacco Leaf)

ashtray by Davidoff.

Chapter

Functional Art: Cigar Ashtrays

Six

Back in the days when smoking was an integral part of almost every adult's lifestyle, ashtrays were what kids made when they wanted to craft a gift for a parent or grandparent. Kids in shop class and at camp hammered sheets of copper, battered plates of tin and shaped and glazed clay into inventive, colorful curios which were treasured by their recipients, and later bequeathed to their makers.

Children, however, were not the only artisans who focused on ashtrays. Dedicated craftspeople and fine artists all devoted time to interpreting the ashtray. They realized that decorators used ashtrays to "anchor" rooms. A well-designed plate might be seen in the dining room on occasion, but a superior ashtray would be displayed day in and day out in almost any room in the house. Even today, one of the smartest moves an aspiring designer can make is to craft an ashtray that will catch people's eyes.

The ashtray, it seems, is making a comeback. Legions of bold smokers are

The world's finest crystal ashtrays vary in style from classically elegant to ornate to art deco to modern. Clockwise from top: The Aster by Hoya Crystal, Cuba by Lalique, the Bristol by Diamond Crown.

insisting that a room is incomplete without distinctive ashtrays. Rumor has it that many designers are applauding the return of the ashtray; they have missed this favorite accessory, one which makes it easy for them to define the focal point of the room.

The cigar ashtray is leading the ashtray renaissance. Cigar ashtrays tend to be bigger than cigarette ashtrays, so designers can make a bolder statement with them. In addition, cigar smokers and the people who buy gifts for them are often willing to invest a bit more for the perfect accessory, so the designers get to work with more expensive materials and develop more sophisticated creations.

The designers aren't completely in control of this renaissance. Cigar smokers are an assertive lot who know their own tastes. As a result, the sheer diversity of the cigar ashtrays seen in fine homes, clubs, and offices is astonishing. Some ashtrays are made from "found objects." We've met a surgeon who, despite his wife's pleas, won't give up his ashtray made from part of a skull. One world traveler hates to use anything but the bowl that was spun out of bubbling lava before his eyes. One waggish woman uses the urn that used to contain her late husband's ashes—she says he would appreciate it. Still another smoker uses the hubcap from his beloved first car.

Objects turned into ashtrays are certainly interesting personal expressions, but often fail as ashtrays. They lack the function, balance, and, to all but the owner, the beauty of ashtrays that were designed as ashtrays. Purchasing, instead of discovering, an ashtray does not limit one's self-expression. No matter what your idea of beauty, someone is crafting marble, brass, steel, glass, or another material, or combination of materials, into a cigar ashtray you will appreciate. In addition, remarkable antique ashtrays can often be found.

The practical requirements for ashtrays are fairly simple. First, they should be fire-resistant and easily cleaned. Some wooden ashtrays, including the ones many of us gouged out of soft pine in shop class and then carefully painted with toxic paints, seem to violate common sense. (Not that there's anything wrong with wooden ashtrays. They can be beautiful, but they should have an easily-cleaned metal or glass inset for catching ashes.) Ashtrays should also be well balanced so they don't spill the ashes at any time, and finished well enough so they don't mar any furniture you put them on.

A cigar ashtray should work as a cigar rest, too. Ashtrays which lack a lip, perch, rest, trough, or other place for the cigar to rest rob the smoker of one of the great pleasures of a well-made and stored cigar: the ability to put the cigar down for a moment, confident that it will stay lit until the next draw. The best ashtrays solidly support the cigar, while leaving the ash suspended over a waiting bowl.

The practical requirements, however, are just the start. It is in the aesthetic realm that better ashtrays excel. A good ashtray contributes not just to the beauty and focus of the room, but also to the beauty and pleasure of the smoking experience.

Many of the best ashtrays are those which capture and reflect the glow at the end of the cigar, as well as the light in the room. A deep-blue porcelain ashtray will appear bright blue in the daylight; when the lights are low, it will darken to a deep-sea blue and reflect the cigar's ash like a pale moon. It is a subtle, but unmistakable, transformation.

Crystal ashtrays are, of course, designed to delight you with their ability to multiply and play with light. Watching a golden glimmer travel from the fireplace in your study through the cuts and facets of a crystal ashtray, and perhaps through a crystal glass of single-malt

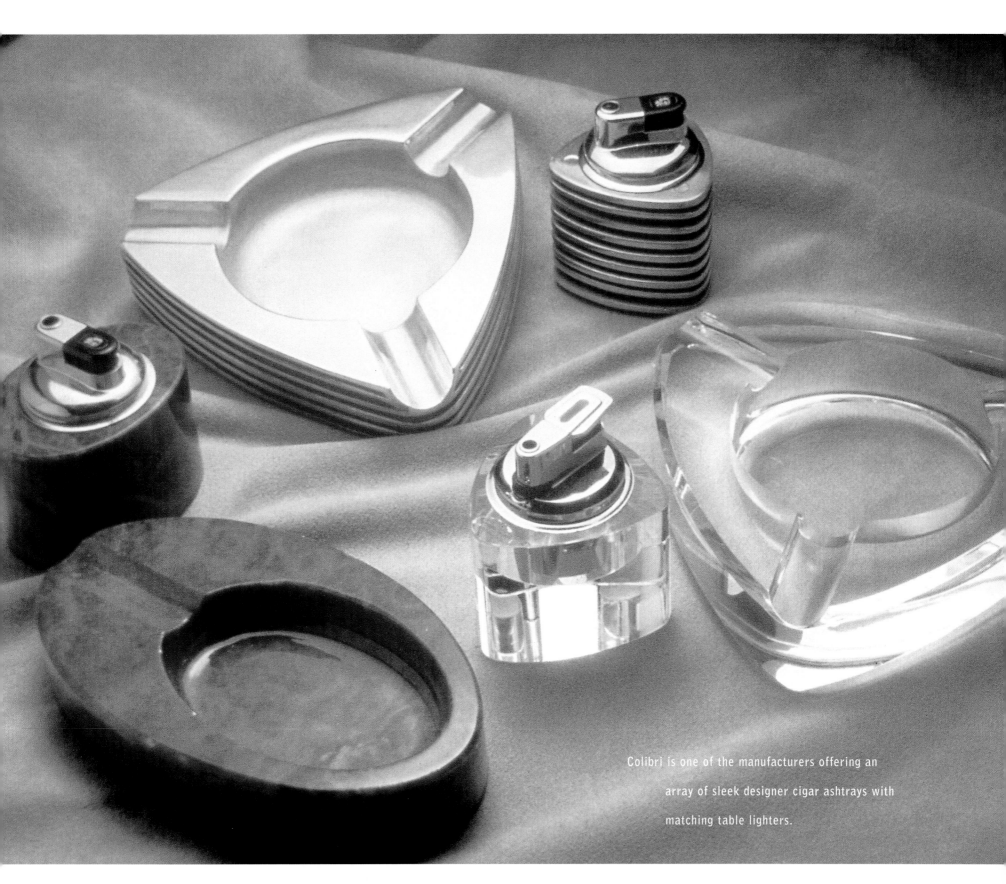

Colibri is one of the manufacturers offering an array of sleek designer cigar ashtrays with matching table lighters.

Ashtray by Perolo made exclusively for the
Cigar Aficionado Collection.

Scotch, is as relaxing as watching a sunset or a rippling brook.

Crystal ashtrays can complement a variety of different decors. Baccarat, the French crystal maker, makes cigar ashtrays to complement table settings which include their famous, exquisite glassware. Lalique's crystal ashtrays are the perfect touch for a salon with an Art Deco feel. Hoya, the Japanese company often associated with fine optical elements, creates innovative crystal artworks which can be the highpoint of a bold, modern office.

Steel is also a popular choice among those seeking an ashtray to crown a modern room. Stainless steel is, of course, functional, but it can also be breathtaking. Brushed steel, molded and bent in surprising shapes and angles, makes a powerful design statement. Aluminum can be used to achieve similar effects.

Other metals, such as copper or brass, can impart a modern or a traditional sense, depending on design and finish. Sailors often like the warmth of brass because it reminds them of the fittings on the yachts they own, or aspire to own. Many smokers appreciate the way the color of copper complements the hues of cigar wrapper leaves.

Stone is, to many, the perfect ashtray material: not likely to burn, and full of the same kind of wondrous natural variations one sees in cigars. Forward-thinking interior architects will ask that some of the stone used for a building's floors or walls be put aside so it can be sculpted into ashtrays which match the building.

Many cigar ashtrays combine materials. Glass ashtrays can have metal inset bowls or be clad in etched gold. Ceramic ashtrays often have wooden bases. Marble ashtrays can have metal fittings, or even plaid beanbag bases. The combinations are limited only by the artist's imagination.

The design of a cigar ashtray is just as important as the materials that are used in making it. Many of the cigar ashtrays on the market today are clearly designed for the solitary smoker. They are generally a modified rectangle with one spot for one cigar in the center. The ultimate in hospitality would be to have enough of these ashtrays so you could provide one for each of your guests.

Unfortunately few people have such resources, so smokers who entertain frequently either have ashtrays designed to accommodate multiple cigars, or have become accustomed to rounding up ashtrays from various rooms before company arrives. There is something wonderfully sociable about ashtrays made for more than a single cigar. They signal that you welcome the company of other smokers.

The last word in sociable ashtrays are the often gigantic, classic floor ashtrays. These standing ashtrays aren't accessories, they are pieces of furniture in their own right. They announce your unquestionable commitment to your smoking pleasure. Luckily, as an unintended consequence of the anti-smoking movement, wonderful old standing ashtrays which once adorned posh hotels, movie theaters, or homes can often be found in antique stores.

These are artworks well worth hunting down and collecting. A curvaceous, green-marble nude holding an ashtray at waist level is a worthy addition to a den. The formally dressed butler proffering a welcome ashtray bespeaks another era. The carved stone sand pit rescued from a bank or municipal building is a relic of a gracious period when time and space both seemed more available.

Standing ashtrays aren't quite as easy to find as they were a few years ago, but you may get lucky scouting in basements and storerooms of old buildings, or asking the construction crew at hotels which are being refurbished. One lucky smoker we met snared an

Churchill's worth of ash, and they are easy to misplace.

But what do you do when you are away from your favorite smoking chair and your favorite, friendly ashtray? Small ashtrays can be tucked into various nooks and crannies of your house so you don't have to feel tethered to one ashtray.

In addition, the portable ashtray can come in handy when you're visiting friends who allow smoking in their home but don't own suitable cigar ashtrays. Not all hosts and hostesses realize that ash can be good for a houseplant or a fine antique rug. (It's true—ask a rug merchant. The ash absorbs oils that otherwise would invade the rug fibers. You can then vacuum out the potentially damaging oils along with the ash.)

The silver-plated, single-cigar ashtrays and holders designed by Adam D. Tihany are fine examples of downsized cigar ashtrays. They include a long perch for the cigar

enormous dragon-carved marble lobby ashtray for the price of hauling it away. He complains about how hard it is to keep his daughter's cat out of the ashtray sand, but he gets little sympathy.

While you are scavenging for standing ashtrays, stay on the lookout for built-in ashtrays, too. The same establishments which had standing ashtrays often had ashtrays incorporated into the walls. A house we visited had ashtrays installed in its bathrooms which had once graced a hotel's elevator lobby.

At the other extreme from the standing ashtray is the small portable ashtray. Small ashtrays are often a poor compromise. It takes too much focus to balance a cigar on them, they don't always hold a

and end in a generous bowl for ash. Other small, portable ashtrays include lids which make it easy to carry the ashes out of the room.

Cigar ashtrays are back, and gift givers everywhere are rejoicing. Brides and grooms include cigar ashtrays in their registries. Retiring executives receive ashtrays with commemorative plaques (and a few cigars, we hope). Most every smoker knows of a spot where they could use an additional ashtray, and most every artisan has an idea for a novel new cigar ashtray design they would like someone to buy or commission.

Who knows? If the ashtray renaissance continues, someday new car models may even have cigar ashtrays, instead of double cup holders.

At left: Trianon Gold ashtray by Hermès St. Louis. This page: Silver-plated cigar ashtrays (and cigar pedestal) designed by Adam D. Tihany for the Villeroy & Boch Signature Collection. From top to bottom: "The Corona," "The Robusto," "The Pedestal," and "The Sobrano."

The English Rose pattern is a reproduction of the one created in 1867 for Eugénie de Montijo, wife of Napoleon III.

Chapter

Fine Art among the Ashes: Porcelain Ashtrays

Seven

The "Folie de Bagatelle" design echoes classic French eighteenth-century architecture, top; "Boston," Bernardaud's creative interpretation of the roaring twenties, bottom.

Europe's top chefs, such as Fredy Girardet of Girardet in Crissier, Switzerland, certainly know what it takes to end a terrific meal: great desserts, perhaps a fine Cognac or Port, and, of course, the world's best cigars. They also understand that, as part of the traditional postprandial experience, a good cigar demands a proper ashtray.

This uncompromising attitude about smoking accouterments is linked to their absolute belief that fine crystal, silver, and china immeasurably enhance the enjoyment of a good dinner. It's all part of what the French call *art de vivre*, the "art of living." This outlook, they would explain, is inextricably linked to, "the art of properly setting a table." For these arbiters of taste, a table isn't properly "dressed" if it doesn't include a *cendrier Havane* from Limoges: that is, a porcelain ashtray made specially to handle an amply proportioned cigar.

So instead of offering just any sort of glass or crystal ashtray, Girardet,

The delicate, interlacing gold-encrusted
swirls elegantly frame the
"Vintimille" ashtray.

whose Michelin three-star restaurant offers a first-class selection of Cuba's finest cigars, goes a step further. To indulge those guests who top off an evening with a great smoke, the restaurant furnishes appropriately oversized Limoges porcelain ashtrays to cradle the cigar and collect its ashes. At Girardet, as at many other two- and three-star establishments, the ashtrays are decorated in the same exclusive motif that graces the restaurant's entire Limoges porcelain dinner service.

To these chefs and other aficionados, there are ashtrays, and then there are ashtrays. Just where you tap that ghostly white cigar ash, after many moments of smoking pleasure, is as much a statement about appreciating the finer things in life as the selection of a good cigar.

Where can you find the world's ultimate ashtrays? The answer, fortunately, is as easy as a first-year French lesson: Limoges (pronounced lee-MOZH).

Located in central France, this slow-paced but agreeable town is known as the cradle of the French porcelain industry; and the ashtrays that artisans produce there, usually part of larger sets of elaborate dinner service, are recognized around the world as the classiest way to cradle a great cigar during a leisurely after-dinner smoke.

That Girardet and other top restaurateurs select Limoges porcelain shouldn't come as a surprise, however. Leading porcelain firms from the city of Limoges, including Bernardaud, de Haviland, and Deshoulières, among others, have been manufacturing fine tableware for Europe's royal houses—not to mention top hotels, restaurants and private clients—for more than 150 years. Indeed, porcelain production in Limoges dates back to the late eighteenth century, according to Michel Bernardaud, director general of Porcelaines Bernardaud, who is himself an avid cigar smoker and someone, of course, who knows a thing or two about l'art de la table and ashtrays.

Bernardaud says that France's oldest continuously operating porcelain producer, Ancienne Manufacture Royale, was founded by the Comte d'Artois in the early 1770s. The Comte d'Artois was the grandson of Louis XV, King of France, hence the "Royale." (In exile, the Comte survived the French Revolution and the turbulent Napoleonic era; later, in 1824, he was crowned Charles X, reigning as king of France from 1825-1830.) Today, Bernardaud, which was founded by Michel's great grandfather, Leonard, and traces its origins to 1863, owns 50 percent of the Ancienne Manufacture Royale, which is operated separately from the family-owned company.

In fact, porcelain making is far older than the Ancienne Manufacture Royale; it's actually an ancient art with roots that can be traced halfway around the world to China. There, according to historical accounts, the production of elaborately designed, clay-fired vases, plates, teapots and the like is a centuries-old tradition. According to art experts, there are some Chinese porcelain vases and bowls that date back to the tenth and eleventh centuries.

One of the world's most celebrated travelers, Marco Polo, is generally credited with being the first to bring Chinese porcelain to Europe following his thirteenth-century voyage across Persia and the Indian subcontinent and through what is present-day China. Marco Polo's porcelaine de Chine became known over time more simply as porcelain, or, in English-speaking countries, as "china." Imitation being the sincerest form of flattery, European artisans tried for years, without success, to reproduce these exotic treasures. Indeed, only after much trial and error would European artisans finally unlock the Orient's jealously guarded techniques of firing the special clay that is used to make fine porcelain.

Above left: Produced for Cartier's exclusive "Louis Cartier" porcelain service, this hexagonal ashtray, left, features a slinking black panther; Above right: Bernardaud's Tuscan-inspired "Borghese" design employs a marquetry motif. Opposite page: in "Balleroy," named for an ancient French forest, the ashtray's black background highlights the rich gold design of mistletoe leaves.

By the early 1700s, after countless experiments using different clay compounds, various firing temperatures, and specially mixed glazes, European artisans and chemists mastered the Asian art of porcelain production. Soon, German, French, and English craftsmen were turning out fine porcelain table services for the leading royal courts throughout Europe. By the late eighteenth century, the most famous centers of porcelain production were Meissen in Germany, Sèvres and Limoges in France, Ginori in Italy, and Royal Worcester and Spode in England.

Given this lineage, porcelain is the true aristocrat of earthenware. In contrast to other types of oven-fired tableware, porcelain is different in three chief ways: it is produced using special clays and compounds; it is oven-fired at much higher temperatures than other types of earthenware; and its decorations, known as glazes, are specially prepared for higher temperatures and, often, are carefully applied by hand.

All Limoges porcelain, like that of its illustrious counterparts in Austria, Britain, Germany, Italy, Japan, and the United States, utilizes a special clay, which is composed of a mixture of kaolin, quartz, and feldspar. These materials are then mixed carefully into a very dense, paste-like substance. The resulting clay is then molded into the appropriate form—a plate, teapot, or ashtray—and baked at about 1,800°F in what is known as the first firing. This first firing process can last as long as eight hours.

After cooling off, the plate, teapot, or ashtray is then dipped in a special enamel bath and immediately undergoes a *grand feu*, or second firing, at about 2,500°F—a process that can last as long as 30 hours. After the grand feu is completed, the decoration process begins. It starts with the application of a design motif, generally through a chromolithographic process, although certain valuable objects are normally painted by hand. In all cases, gold and platinum work on

Produced by the Ancienne
Manufacture Royale,
the "Feuille de Vigne,"
is a spirited toast to
the art of winemaking.

porcelain is hand-painted. A final series of firings, depending on the piece and the decorations, is then undertaken, at temperatures ranging from about 1,500°F to 2,200°F.

Porcelaines Bernardaud's ashtrays are generously proportioned. The ashtrays also exhibit great personality, since many of Bernardaud's designs are inspired by artists like Kees Van Dongen, Raymond Loewy, and Bernard Buffet. But many of the trademark Bernardaud designs come from the company's own atelier.

A famous example of Bernardaud's own work is its "Boston" design, a somewhat dreamy, but definitely jazzy, interpretation of the "Roaring Twenties." Conceived and designed in Bernardaud's own atelier in 1925, "Boston" features a multicolored confetti look against an elegant gold background.

Echoing the sophisticated look of the '30s, Bernardaud's "Paris" design reflects the Art Deco style inspired by the French artists Sonia Delauney and Fernand Leger. The ashtray's brilliant white background contrasts dramatically with exotic-looking women posed against a colorful background of powdered gold, soft coral and vivid turquoise.

Jean-Pierre Hamard, artistic director of Bernardaud's atelier, oversees all the firm's design work, from the revival of historic designs of eighteenth-century French porcelain to new creative work by contemporary French designers like Catherine Bergen and Italian painters such as Giovanna Amoruso. In all, Porcelaines Bernardaud releases almost 20 new designs a year, not including special orders for clients like the sultan of Oman, Air France, and foreign embassies, among others.

In addition to this special-order work, Bernardaud also produces a luxurious porcelain service for Cartier. One set includes a splendid series of ashtrays, one of which has an unusual but colorful hexagonal shape, featuring a slinking black panther. The ashtray, which comes in three other sizes, is part of Cartier's exclusive "Louis Cartier" porcelain service.

A classic nineteenth-century design was completed at the request of Empress Eugènie Marie de Montijo de Guzmán, Napoleon III's wife, a Spanish aristocrat, who was known for her exquisite (and expensive) tastes. The porcelain set was commissioned by the empress in 1867 and designed in an English-style rose motif. The pattern, called Eugènie de Montijo, was a great success at court, and is still in use at Hôtel de Palais, originally Empress Eugènie's summer palace, and since 1883, one of the world's great luxury hotels.

The choice among cigar ashtrays has never been better, says Bernardaud. He knows, as do other confirmed cigar smokers, that after a cozy dinner at a cigar-friendly restaurant or at home, there is no better place to cradle your cigar than in a beautiful porcelain ashtray. That's what the French would call "living with style."　　　—DAVID L. ROSS

See caption, page 84.

Chapter Eight

Artistry in Small Packages: Cigar-Box Art

The recent upsurge of interest in cigar-box connoisseurship has combined with the glitter and excitement of celebrity artists to create a mini-movement within the contemporary art world. This development, sometimes called "Cig Art," involves the creation of cigar boxes which have been painted, sculpted, encrusted, or otherwise decorated by some of the most renowned visual artists of the day. Artists who have risen to the challenge of the new medium include such luminaries as Red Grooms, Roy Lichtenstein, Kenny Scharf, Robert Indiana, Audrey Flack, Janet Fish, Wolf Kahn, Will Barnet, Patrick Brady, Sandro Chia, Andres Serrano, David Lynch, Milton Glaser, Mihail Chemiaken, Sheila Abzug, Shannon Brady, LeRoy Neiman, and Emily Mason.

Cig Art represents the extension of a cigar-box art tradition that dates back at least to the European Post-Impressionists. Among the artists who gathered in the small harbor town of Pont-Aven in northwest France

TOP RIGHT: Tramp art jewelry box on pedestal stand, circa 1890. The main compartment is a cigar box. BOTTOM LEFT: A pineapple finial tops this Ziggurat-style box with seven drawers and a lift-top compartment. Made entirely from cigar boxes.

during the late 1880s, were Paul Gaugin and a young friend and colleague named Paul Serusier. The two were interested in using heightened color intensities and flattened three-dimensional shapes to create abstract representations of the natural world around them—an art movement that later became known as "Synthetism." One of Serusier's early Synthetist works is "The Talisman," a small "abstract landscape" painted on a cigar-box lid.

Tramp Art, a form of American folk art, was another early expression of interest in the cigar box as an art medium. So named from the romantic notion that its makers were wandering hobos who bartered their creations for food and lodging, Tramp Art was made primarily from wooden cigar boxes. Common features include the stacking of diminishing shapes to form pyramids, and the notching or chip-carving of edges with a simple knife. Surviving pieces, which date from the 1870s through the 1930s, vary in form from jewelry boxes to picture frames to articles of furniture.

Following the heyday of Tramp Art, the tradition of cigar-box art lay relatively fallow for a number of years awaiting the cigar renaissance. The new Cig Art has most recently and formally been celebrated at annual gala benefits hosted by *Cigar Aficionado* magazine, the National Arts Club, and the Visual Arts Foundation, among others. The brainchild of artist Patrick Brady and art patron Rick Nulman, these Cig Art benefits have introduced the art world to over one hundred new pieces, including the works depicted here.

PAGE 80 KATHLEEN BARTOLETTI The theme of this piece, entitled "Queen of Darts," is the pain of love. On the lid of the box is a miniature dartboard bearing the figure of a young woman who tries, in vain, to protect her heart by folding her hands across her chest. Her image is adapted from the painting "Le printemps" (The Return of Spring), by the French painter Adolphe-William Bouguereau. A decorative border around the side of the box incorporates a playing card motif; on one side, the cards depict a straight of hearts, while on the other, they hold a combination of aces and eights known as "the dead man's hand."   1 SUSUMU SATO "As Dostoyevsky said, 'Beauty shall save the world.' I have always been inspired by beauty, especially the beauty of the human form. The relationship between the cigar and the human form is so evident that it seemed just natural to utilize photographs of the Lavender Twins to compliment such a classic receptacle as the cigar box."   2 PATRICK BRADY "My art explores the co-mingling of the various races and ethnicities that comprise the United States' mosaic. I've interpreted the flag's red and white stripes as the intertwining limbs of Americans of all colors. The flag's traditional stars have been re-interpreted as the lips and voices of the public in celebration of democracy."   3 SABINE MIGLAR "When I paint, I aim to convey simple and strong graphical representations of archetypes that resonate within all of humanity. As with this cigar box, the four elements—fire, water, earth and air—seek union with the male and female principals of yin and yang; thus representing humankind and nature merged."   4 MIHAIL CHEMIAKIN The box is designed as a field report from a Russian spy describing the characteristics of tobacco, which the spy considers a new secret weapon. Included in the box and its two secret dispatches are portraits and descriptions of key players in the tobacco industry, diagrams and botanical analyses of the tobacco plant, and samples of tobacco.

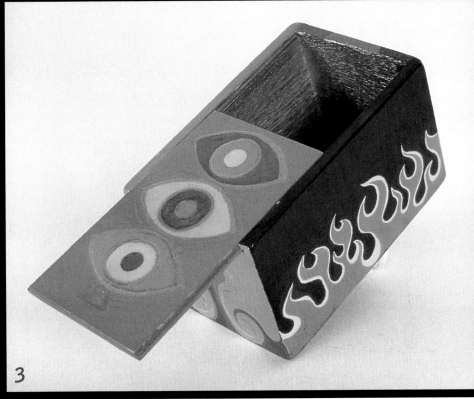

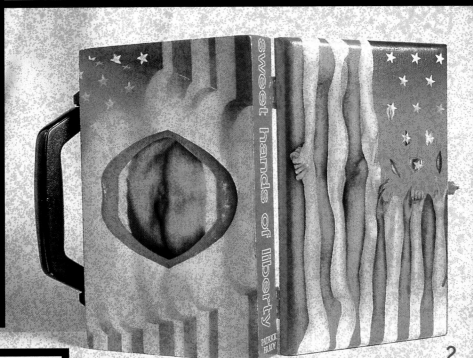

85

5 MARSHALL ARISMAN "Monkeys have always been perfect subjects for artists to mirror human behavior. Sacred monkeys in particular have fascinated me and I have devoted the better part of the past year to working on a series of paintings and sculptures about them. By the way, [in the artworks] they all smoke and usually they smoke cigars."

6 SHANNON BRADY "I grew up enjoying the works of the eighteenth-century English satirists and twentieth-century German Expressionists and have found my own fascination with the social interaction and emotional makeup of people around me. Spending several years in bars, clubs, theaters, restaurants, and pool halls has given me insight, material, and inspiration to paint the fashionable and social follies of those seeking some sort of strange personal fulfillment and entertainment. I see life as a comical circus filled with lust, love, sorrow, depression, happiness, envy, greed, and self-absorbed posturing."

7 CASSANDRA LOZANO "My drawings and their sculptural frames portray surreal beings in trompe l'oeil environments acting out a variety of myths and stories of my own invention . . . inspired by mythology, [the paintings of] Arcimboldo, Spanish vanitas artwork, and votive, fetish, fertility, and folk objects. I use a broad spectrum of carpentry and decorative craft techniques . . . inspired by Adirondack furniture, Mexican tin punched objects, Haitian sequined voodoo banners, African gilded wood carvings, [folk artist] Rodia's Watt Towers, folk painting, and kitsch objects. The lighting and opulent surface treatments of my sculptures harken back to parade floats."

8 ROY LICHTENSTEIN

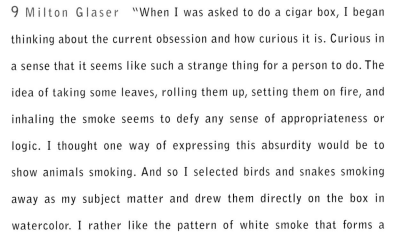

9

11

9 Milton Glaser "When I was asked to do a cigar box, I began thinking about the current obsession and how curious it is. Curious in a sense that it seems like such a strange thing for a person to do. The idea of taking some leaves, rolling them up, setting them on fire, and inhaling the smoke seems to defy any sense of appropriateness or logic. I thought one way of expressing this absurdity would be to show animals smoking. And so I selected birds and snakes smoking away as my subject matter and drew them directly on the box in watercolor. I rather like the pattern of white smoke that forms a counterpoint to the dark shapes of the animals and gives a decorative quality to the surface."

10 LeRoy Neiman "My cigar box decor pays homage to the great movie idol Clark Gable, who manned a cigar with such masculinity and style. While serving my cigar-smoking apprenticeship in my teens, puffing on five-cent Harvesters, White Owls, and an occasional 10-cent Dutch Master, I looked to Clark's films for the form, as it was he who set the standard I fancied."

11 Sandro Chia "The other day I was smoking a cigar with Mr. Oscar Wilde. Between [one] puff and the other he told me, "To smoke a cigar is a complete pleasure that leaves you unsatisfied.'"

12 Sheila Abzug — Rural Tracery 1997. The bucolic idyll of rural America or the old-world charm of European cityscapes are the focus of the paintings of Sheila Abzug. In this work, a tree falls, lending its substance to the panel upon which the artist molds her oil paints into the essence of the tree. The cigar box vista, complete in five dimensions, encloses the contents of the distant barn.

Chapter

The Art of the Sale: Cigar Advertisements

Nine

Consider a 1950 ad in *The New York Times* for El Producto cigars. The half-page advertisement shows a forlorn man doubled over with grief. His psychiatrist, leaning back and smiling while smoking an El Producto, diagnoses the man's malady. "He is a victim of frustration," the psychiatrist says. "He has been abroad where he cannot buy El Producto." Next to pictures of the cigars, the copy reads: "No psychiatrist needed—try a pocketful of El Productos today."

Another ad from the same period shows three men in smart suits and Stetsons at the racetrack smoking "America's Number One Cigar, the New Phillies." These pricey gems were 12 cents apiece—3 for 35 cents!—and were a vast improvement over their Philly predecessors because of their "richer Havana tobacco," "finer wrapper," and "milder smoking" (due, but of course, to "the patented curing and mellowing process" used to make them). "Yessiree!" one of the three says, "when I want real downright

smoking pleasure my money goes to Phillies every time." Tucked into the *Times* sports pages, ads for Admiration cigars and Gold Label Bonitas are equally as spirited and innocent.

The 1950s represent a turning point in the style of cigar advertising. During the previous 100 years, cigar ads were among the best-conceived, -written and -illustrated of all product advertisements, with wordplay, exciting images, and graphic magnificence. Ads since 1950, however, are for the most part less imaginative and colorful. The spot "Should a Gentleman Offer a Tiparillo to a Lady?" (1961), memorable for its jingle, is a notable exception.

Just ask John Grossman. Author, painter, graphic artist, and collector, Grossman owns a firm called The Gifted Line that includes more than 225,000 museum-quality antique images. He labels his collection "graphic ephemera" and displays his wares in Point Richmond, California. Included in his collection are more than 85,000 cigar box labels and more than 5,000 other items related to the cigar industry: bands, proof sheets, show cards, posters—even cigar trading cards. For researchers and historians, no more colorful and plentiful record of cigar-related print items exists anywhere.

How did Grossman become interested in cigar ephemera? "Ephemera have wonderful vitality," he says "Cigar ads were always beautifully illustrated. Labels themselves were printed in anywhere from eight to 10 colors. Each cigar manufacturer tried to top the others."

And how. In the latter half of the nineteenth century, commercial color printing was a novelty, and cigar manufacturers made the most of it. In an attempt to appeal to a broad audience, many of the early ads depict cigars in a manly, sporting context.

One cigar box label (1878) shows a cigar-smoking frog hitting a red, white, and blue ball. Other frogs—non-smoking frogs, that is—wait to catch it. The ad doesn't suggest a brand name. The only copy reads "The Hit." The illustration is vibrant, homey, even patriotic, with the multicolored ball and an American flag placed in the outfield. The artwork is exquisite.

Other sporting ads were real grabbers. The Bruiser cigar box label (1886) shows a bloody fist surrounded by a boxing ring—and that's it. No cigar is in the fist. The dramatic image suggests that if you don't smoke Bruiser—a "real man's brand"—you'll be going down for the count.

Tobacco trading cards were another hit. Stacks of trading cards might be given by the manufacturer to the retailer, who passed them out to customers. People often saved the cards, putting them in scrapbooks. The cards had some attention-grabbing image on one side and information about the product on the flip side.

Capadura Cigar trading cards from 1885 show baseball players in assorted poses. Baseball players were America's sporting heroes in the 1880s, and these colorful Capadura drawings show muscle men in the flashy baseball attire of the day. "A Short Stop!" hollers one image, showing a ballplayer getting his mouth bloodied, presumably by a batted ball. Another slugger has the brand name Capadura on his bat, and the copy

reads, "Two Men Out and Three Men on Base!" In a real pinch, the implication goes, Capaduras will come through.

Capadura did not go unchallenged. In what may have been the first instance of combative cigar advertising, the Imperial Cigar Manufacturer in 1885 printed on one of its trading cards the following challenge: "$10,000 REWARD for a genuine CAPADURA SEGAR/ Not Clear Havana Filled/ DEALERS ONLY SUPPLIED." The challenge implies that the Capaduras—far from being made of the finest tobacco—are impostors. The challenge was printed in the same stark fashion reserved for criminal "Wanted" posters in post offices.

While smokes like Capaduras and Bruisers clearly speak to the common man, other cigars made their pitch to different classes.

"Smoke Housekeeper Cigars" shouts one 1885 show card ad. The housekeeper is a voluptuous woman in a low-cut dress who graces the center of the ad. Images to the right and left show her pinning a flower to a man's lapel and stooping provocatively to light his cigar. The message is unmistakably sexual; the buxom housekeeper, like the cigar by that name, caters to your pleasure.

Another brand that called out to men of leisure was the Elkton Bouquet cigar. An 1896 cigar box label showed ten men in formal wear relaxing after dinner. Some drink Champagne and others smoke while a box of Elktons sits opened on the dinner table.

Cigar manufacturers also tried to associate their products with images of progress. A locomotive labeled "The Iron Horse" appears on one cigar box label from 1885. No one is smoking and there isn't even a hint of the brand name of this cigar. But the new and powerful locomotive reminded people of progress and reliability." The price of below the ad reads "$20,000 for 1,000, $2.20 per 100." The cigar was made by Schumacher and Ettlinger on Bleecker Street in New York.

Ethel Barrymore and other glamorous people made appearances on cigar paraphernalia, as well. Lillian Russell and Queen Victoria were on labels, even though Queen Victoria was staunchly opposed to cigars.

A 1922 wall calendar features the Marie Antoinette cigar. "Par excellence," the copy reads. Why? Because this brand is "filled with the Vuelta Havana's Choicest Tobacco." What Cuban tobacco had to do with a decapitated queen of France is unclear.

Other ads are so odd they defy categorization. One 1905 brand name was called Rotten. "Rotten. But What's in a Name?" the copy asks. (We wonder: Is the taste rotten? The smell?) The word "but" appears on the butt end, while the rest of the tobacco has been reduced to ash.

A 1910 show card depicts a large owl driving an open car. The brand name is "Owl" and the implication is that the cigar in question, like the vigilant nocturnal creature that bears its name, is a wise choice. A beautifully colored 1910 show card shows a rooster puffing a Tampa Fad. "5 cents," begins the copy. But, the ad continues, Tampa Fads are "worth any money."

While more recent pitches for Dutch Masters, Roi-Tans, and El Productos have graphic elements worth noting, the best cigar ads have clearly come and gone by the time 1950 arrives. But the older ads still resonate with meaning. Illustrators and printers had to capture the flavor of the times, and advertising, every bit as much as art, can evoke an era and its people. —KEN SHOULER

The traditional cigar-store Indian expresses an
air of dignity.

Chapter
Ten

Standing Tall: Cigar-Store Indians

This zinc Indian chief by William Demuth, circa 1885, typifies the quintessential "Indian" look commonly garnered by carvers from printed illustrations, preconceptions and prevailing stereotypes of the nineteenth century.

Once they stood guard on the sidewalks of America, as familiar and unremarkable as policemen and lampposts. Sturdy, noble, common, and unthreatening, the cigar-store Indian was an intrinsic part of the commercial landscape, taking its place alongside other visual clues to the merchandise in the stores with which they were associated. For some 50 years, from about 1840 to 1890, they stood mutely, their wooden fists offering wooden cigars.

Cigar-store Indians, along with a cast of other characters, faded from view at the turn of the century. As electric lighting became more available and other inventions of the twentieth century made their appearance, the practice of putting representations of half-naked Native Americans on modern city streets fell out of favor. Because the cigar-store Indians were not quite art—proper sculptures were made of marble or bronze, not ephemeral wood—few mourned their loss.

Yet long before Madison Avenue became a synonym for advertising—and then an epithet for hucksterism—the men who carved these figures summarized their craft as "the image business."

Designed to entice customers into a tobacco store, the carvings—not just Indians, but other ethnic figures and historical personages as well—often included standardized, instantly recognizable features, which to the modern eye often embody offensive stereotypes. The cigar-store sculptures were part of the era's practice of establishing visual clues to a store's merchandise. Huge eyeglass frames and outsized gloves, hats, and shoes were among the items represented in three dimensions and hung near shop doors in the nineteenth century. (The theory that most people at the time were illiterate and couldn't read printed signs is a notion as stereotyped as the figures themselves. The sculptures were simply part of a popular advertising tradition.)

But why associate Indians with cigar shops? Harken back to your primary school history lessons and there's an indelible image of the Indians offering a peace pipe to the Pilgrims. The connection between Indians and tobacco was so clear and strong to the nineteenth-century smoker that the figures were readily understood to represent the tobacco and smoking paraphernalia that were available in the shop. Using Indians to promote cigar smoking would scarcely be the first choice in our age of political correctness, but that is not a problem for those who lovingly collect these figures.

The idea of using Indians to promote the sale of tobacco is attributed to the British. (As early as 1598, a German traveler noted that "the English are constantly smoking tobacco.") In England, the American Indian had become a symbol for North America, and even for the entire New World. Although the carved figures first appeared in England, and then elsewhere in Europe, an untold number—estimated at tens of thousands—were eventually made in the United States and Canada.

Drawing upon printed illustrations, their own preconceptions, and the prevailing stereotypes, the carvers whipped up figures that reinforced those very stereotypes. Hence the "noble savage," usually representing no particular tribe, personified the idea of a primitive being who nevertheless had lofty thoughts. In dressing the figures, the carvers used their own imaginations to create a white man's idea of a quintessentially "Indian" look. The clothing was delicately draped, billowy, and soft in appearance. In practice, the result was sometimes more like a Roman toga than a buckskin.

There is a definite air of unreality about the figures, like carousel horses that evoke children's fairy-tale figures rather than the flesh and blood solidity of the living animal. Although the Indians stand next to you on the sidewalk, they seem to have their eyes fixed firmly on the horizon, as if they might be looking toward the nearest sea. Indeed, many of them were made of white pine taken from sections of ships' masts, and almost all carvers of cigar-store Indians came out of the ship-carving tradition. As the demand for wooden ships diminished, the carvers had to take their skills elsewhere.

Although eight-out-of-ten cigar-store figures were modeled as Indians, anything else connected with tobacco or smoking was fair game for the carvers. Other popular ethnic types included the kilted Scotsman known for his snuff, and the Turk in his exotic garb. (It is worth noting that these stereotypes were solidly established long before Hollywood began portraying Indians and foreigners according to hastily sketched national characteristics.)

A wooden cigar-store Indian stands watch in front of
New York's University Cigar Emporium, circa 1895.

Designed to entice customers into a tobacco store, the carvings often included figures other than the Indian. Clockwise from top left: "Manz's Minstrel," a "Blackmoor," circa 1870; Indian maiden figure, circa 1888–1903; "The Little Navigator," circa 1810; "General Butler," circa 1880.

In addition, some cigar shop figures were fashioned as "blackamoors," another stereotype that owes its origins to England. The blackamoor, or African boy, was generally portrayed in a minstrel costume or other glad rags and usually sported an impossibly wide grin with enormous white teeth. The figure derived from British associations with Africa as a place of extreme exoticism.

Another general type which carvers sometimes took as their subject was the Fur Trapper: a figure originally attributed to the German-American carver Julius Melchers. Melchers worked in Detroit, where fur trapping would have been a familiar occupation, and trappers were among the most rugged, romantic figures of their day. Sailors were popular as well—a natural choice for carvers who came from the ship-carving tradition.

To accomplish their objective of attracting customers to the stores, the carvers used many well-known fictional and real characters of the day. The novels of James Fenimore Cooper inspired figures, as did Minnehaha from Longfellow's poem "Song of Hiawatha." Buffalo Bill was a popular subject, and so was George Fox, a pantomimist who created the character of Humpty Dumpty. Only someone with a wide reputation would be suitable as a cigar-store figure, since the association had to be made at a glance.

The decline of the carved figures can be traced to several circumstances, including the passage of laws against figures blocking sidewalks. But there were two primary factors that sealed their fate. First, the ship carvers who had turned to creating such figures simply died off; as the wooden sailing ship was replaced by metal-hulled ships after the Civil War, the era of trained carvers came to an end. Second, and equally important, advertising fashions changed. Store-front figures were increasingly seen as symbols of the past, as old-fashioned. Taking their place were techniques such as color lithography, as the emphasis in advertising began to shift to graphics.

The figures lingered on here and there. Even into the 1940s and 1950s, a lone figure could be spotted on the streets of some cities, including New York, but time took its toll. The paint used had to be continually renewed, victim to the ravages of weather. Those that survived became landmarks in their neighborhoods, reminders of a more colorful urban past.   —ETTAGALE BLAUER

Nearly all of the world's most princely residences built in the nineteenth century embraced the newfound conceit of a separate enclave for smoking, drinking, leisure pursuits, and man talk. Some of the rooms that took on such dual functions include billiard rooms, hunting rooms, and libraries, such as the one shown here in the Kingscote Mansion in Newport, Rhode Island.

Chapter

A Place of Distinction: Smoking Parlors

Eleven

Grandeur was not a standard in American homes when Ruggles Sylvester Morse set out, in 1858, to build himself a show house in Portland, Maine. Still, Morse, a successful hotelier in New Orleans, did not search far for inspiration. Already quite familiar to him were the closest things to palaces that the country had: the grand hotels of the day. From these models he cribbed the notion that his house should be filled with public spaces which utilized the most modern creature comforts of the day, such as central heating, running water, and toilets. Also, there must be a smoking room to which gentlemen could repair to enjoy cigars.

The smoking room that he built, an exotic Turkish-style retreat with Moorish arabesques, fresco-painted in vivid red and green, is considered the country's earliest existing domestic smoking parlor. Morse built his home, now called Victoria Mansion, on the cusp of an era that would produce scores of the world's most princely residences—nearly all of them

George Washington Vanderbilt's commodious estate, Biltmore (see photo page 111) contained an entire "bachelor's wing" where guests could smoke in the billiards room (shown here), the smoking parlor (see photo page 110), or the gun room.

embracing the newfound conceit of a separate enclave for smoking, drinking, leisure pursuits, and man talk.

Located in a second-floor tower (fashion would later place the typical smoking parlor on the ground level), Morse's smoking room was small (10 feet by 10 feet) but dazzling. A divan and two ottomans made of cherry wood were upholstered in the same silk-and-wool Islamic weave that was used for the curtains and valances. Imported from England, a five-light gasolier, which was suspended by a system of weights and pulleys that allowed it to be easily raised and lowered, might have been used for lighting cigars as well as illumination.

The room would have easily served the social function of separating the genders—it was, after all, a time when smoking in the presence of a lady was considered extremely impolite. But, judging from the extent of the decor, the scope of Morse's intent was much greater. Some said that he wanted the entire house to be an advertisement for the way he made his money.

Interior designer Gustave Herter helped Morse advance the cause of the smoking parlor by setting standards and style. The German-born Herter was one of the first professional interior designers in America and was highly renowned in the world of luxury hotels (where he more than likely met Morse). He would go on, in partnership with his brother Christian, to form Herter Brothers, a name synonymous with the opulent style of the Gilded Age. It was Herter who directed the ornamentation of Victoria Mansion and constructed the smoking room's furniture. He probably chose the motif because of the fine tobaccos (and possibly some more exotic smoking materials) that came from Turkey.

This style, also called Islamic or Moorish because of other Near Eastern influences, epitomized the first smoking rooms in the United States. One practical design consideration was the use of sliding pocket doors, which in the absence of good ventilation were meant to trap the smoke within the room. In later homes, improved air circulation, rather than confinement, would be the strategy for dealing with tobacco odors.

Styles would change and smoking parlors would enlarge as they took on such dual functions as billiards rooms, libraries, or hunting rooms, but Herter had helped to describe a new direction in which interior designers could make a statement.

Newport, Rhode Island, captures the spirit of the Gilded Age with its concentration of grandiose "cottages;" The Breakers, above, was the largest. Cigars were smoked in the splendor of the billiard room, left, with its walls of Cippolino marble and carved alabaster arches.

When industrialist George Merritt doubled the size of Lyndhurst mansion, below, in Tarrytown, New York he installed an inner sanctum in the library, right, where he could enjoy cigars as well as books.

Most of the great mansions in the United States were built during an era of conspicuous spending that spanned from the 1870s until just before the First World War. The period would be called the "Gilded Age," after the title of a contemporary novel co-authored by Mark Twain. Great wealth was consolidated among a fortunate few, who thought of themselves as "nature's noblemen." (Outside the fold they would be referred to as "robber barons.") The aristocratic metaphors were not unfounded, as these men built temples to themselves that would rival the palaces of Europe. Writers such as Henry James and Edith Wharton developed a love/hate fascination with these play-

grounds that the author Louis Auchincloss would later describe as "crudely crammed with gold."

Through the efforts of preservation groups across the country, many of these American castles are being maintained and may be visited by aficionados eager to vicariously experience the almost incomprehensible luxury in which cigars were enjoyed a century ago.

The oceanside town of Newport, Rhode Island includes some of the most spectacular mansions ever built. Towards the end of the nineteenth century, this playground of the extravagantly rich would witness one of the most pretentious periods of competitive home building of all time, spearheaded by men such as the Vanderbilts, the Astors, Stuyvesant Fish, James Gordon Bennett, and Oliver Hazard Belmont. But because the owners aimed to recreate English or French architecture and design of the Renaissance and the sixteenth to eighteenth centuries, they left little room for fresh ideas—except in the smoking parlor. There were no historical precedents until the nineteenth century for smoking rooms, so their design became all the more innovative and, in many cases, exotic.

Social conventions in this rarefied circle became so rigid that the taking of tobacco was often written into the rules of behavior. Mrs. Beeton's *Book of Household Management*, a primer on the average mistress's duties in the late nineteenth century, included a section titled "The Proper Conduct Upon Leaving the Dinner Table" which described the customs that revolved around that part of life:

"When fruit has been taken and a glass or two of wine passed round, the time will have arrived when the hostess . . . rises and gives her guests the signal to retire to the drawing room. The gentlemen will rise at the same time. The one nearest the door opens it for the ladies, all courteously standing until the last lady has withdrawn. In former times [the mid-nineteenth century], when the bottle circulated freely among the guests, the ladies retired earlier than they do at present times. Thanks, however, to the changes time has wrought, moderation is now invariable amongst gentleman and they now take but a brief interval for tobacco, talk, and coffee in the smoking or billiard room before they rejoin the ladies."

In the Gilded Age, great wealth presented a kind of entrapment for ladies and gentlemen, who were expected to follow a social schedule laid out almost to the minute. In the case of Newport, it was very much a female-dominated environment. In July and August, wives would take up residence in these grand houses, which were considered something like summer cottages by their affluent owners. Husbands, too busy building empires to fully enjoy the fruits of their labor, joined them mostly on weekends or for a few days of vacation. They commuted from New York or Boston by train or steamer and hurried to fit sporting diversions into the 'round-the-clock social whirl.

Gentlemen who were in town might spend their day in athletic pursuits such as yachting, fishing, hunting, riding or driving horses, golfing, and playing tennis. Little time was spent at home. If they wanted a cigar they probably went to the Reading Room, an exclusive men's club that remains private today, where they could engage in confabulation without fear of offending ladies with either their smoking or their bawdy talk. In the evening, they were expected to escort their wives. (In the absence of a husband, one of the young officers from the nearby naval college could stand in his stead.)

So although these men bankrolled great smoking parlors, they spent precious little time in them, except after dinner parties, and

even then very briefly. The disappearance of that men for the rest of the evening to enjoy cigars and brandy without their wives was a European custom that didn't travel well to the United States. It was considered un-American to abandon your wife.

The amount of cash sunk into erecting Newport "cottages" was simply staggering. Whereas Victoria Mansion cost the then-princely sum of $100,000, by 1892 William Kissam Vanderbilt, son of William Henry and grandson of the Commodore, had built Newport's Marble House, based on the Petit Trianon at Versailles, for $11 million. By the end of the century, the owners in Newport seemed to be playing a game of "my mansion is bigger than your mansion," and the homes showed it in every detail.

Among the eight properties dating from 1748 to 1902 that may be toured in Newport, four are revivalist mansions: two built by Vanderbilt heirs, one by the steamship owner Hermann Oelrichs, and the other by coal magnate Edward J. Berwind. They represent only the tip of the iceberg, however. At one point there were as many as 50 of these vainglorious mansions in the small city.

More modest, but still breathtakingly lavish, are two houses from the middle part of the century, one done in Gothic and the other in Victorian style.

The Gothic-style Kingscote, which was built in 1839, was sold to William Henry King, a trader with China, in 1863. Though King was committed to a mental hospital in 1866 (where records show he continued to receive shipments of imported cigars), his nephew, David, continued his uncle's tradition of decorating with objects imported from China. He began upgrading the rustic house to the new formality of Newport in 1878, adding a parlor-full of overstuffed Turkish

furniture from the New York design firm of Lèon Marcotte, including sofas and chairs in rose damask. He later commissioned a three-story addition by Stanford White, the architect who, with his partners McKim and Meade, would go a long way toward defining the buildings of the Gilded Age.

One of the most remarkable properties in the United States is George Washington Vanderbilt's Biltmore Mansion, above. The ambitious estate near Asheville, North Carolina, is believed to be the largest privately owned home in the United States. The "bachelor's wing" contained not only a smoking room, opposite, but a library, gun room, billiard room (page 105), and private rooms for un-attached male guests, who could move easily from their chambers to the men's enclave.

The Newport County Preservation Society is also custodian to Chateau-Sur-Mer, a Victorian built in 1852 for William S. Wetmore, who also made his fortune in the China trade. His son, George Peabody Wetmore, who would later serve as governor of Rhode Island, inherited the house and commissioned Richard Morris Hunt in 1871 to renovate it, reflecting design concepts then fashionable in Europe. (Hunt, another principal architect of the Gilded Age, would go on to design 25 mansions and cottages in Newport and several along New York's Fifth Avenue, most with distinctive smoking rooms.) In Wetmore's mansion there are two pieces of particular interest to smokers: a Chinese-style lacquer cigar box made in the 1840s and emblazoned with the Wetmore coat of arms, and an owl-shaped humidor.

Given the scale of the truly great mansions of Newport, which were so much grander than anything that came before them in America, only a few architects were up to the task of designing them. These designers, in turn, fully developed their skills as a result of all the consistent work. Hunt became almost the family architect to the Vanderbilts, while McKim, Meade, and White (cigar smokers all) picked up much of the rest of the business.

As the revivalist trend took over, the smoking room began to appear as a dual-purpose room, incorporating billiards, hunting motifs, or the library into the concept of the male domain. Novelist Wharton and designer Ogden Codman had this to say in their 1897 treatise, *The Decoration of Houses*:

"The smoking-room proper, with its *mise en scène* of Turkish divans, narghilehs, brass coffee-trays, and other Oriental properties, is no longer considered a necessity in the modern house; and the room which would formerly have been used for this special purpose now comes rather under the head of the master's lounging-room or 'den'—since the latter word seems to have attained the dignity of a technical term."

The two self-appointed purveyors of style go on to preach the wisdom of practicality in furnishing such a room. Their concept apparently informed such rooms as the neo-Byzantine billiards parlor at The Breakers, which was built in 1895 from a Hunt design in the style of a sixteenth-century Italian palace. The room was decorated by Tiffany and Baumgarten, with portraits, a formidable desk, and a billiards table, and it had a high ceiling and lofty windows for ventilation. Just off the dining room, the room entailed but a short walk for gentlemen seeking their postprandial cigar and billiards.

It is probable that in some of the other great mansions that survive today—like Oelrichs' Rosecliff (1902), designed by White; Berwind's The Elms (1901), designed by Horace Trumbauer; and William K. Vanderbilt's Marble House (1892), designed by Hunt—the library may have been used for the purpose of cigar smoking. At The Elms, an alabaster humidor remains as part of the furniture collection.

Many of the grand homes that were built closer to New York City and used as regular residences, such as those along the Hudson River and on Long Island, also employed the library or a den for cigar smoking. Lyndhurst, a Gothic Revival mansion in Tarrytown, New York, is a good example. Built in 1838 in a region north of New York City which had been romanticized by the Hudson River School of artists and would acquire several grand mansions of its own, the home was acquired in 1864 by George Merritt, a holder of a patent for railroad car springs. He would enlarge the building in keeping with the era's new scale of entertainment, with designs by the original architect, Alexander Jackson Davis.

The library, which had originally been a dining room, was

enlarged, creating an inner sanctum out of the serving bay. Called the cabinet room, it is where Merritt most likely enjoyed his cigars, as well as his books. Furnishings included a large pierced-oak Gothic Revival armchair and a marble mantelpiece. Davis designed furniture for use throughout the house that echoed the Gothic appointments of the building's exterior. Furniture from the Herter Brothers can also be found there. The original library, on the second story, became a lavish art gallery.

Railroad tycoon Jay Gould bought Lyndhurst in 1880. The property is now part of the National Trust for Historic Preservation, having been bequeathed by Gould's daughter in 1961.

Further up the Hudson, in Hyde Park, is Frederick Vanderbilt's mansion. Built in 1898, it is a magnificent example of the Beaux Arts style. Inside the enormous building, Vanderbilt took his cigars either in the den just off the main hall or in the room where he kept guns and hunting trophies, against a backdrop of heavy wood ornamentation. Among the mansion's celebrated guests were Franklin Roosevelt (whose own home was just up the street), various royalty, and Winston Churchill, who no doubt enjoyed a cigar or two in the den. Vanderbilt left two humidors to the collection that has been run by the National Park Service since 1940; a cigar is kept in the den to indicate that he probably always had smokes at hand.

Aside from New York City and the playgrounds of the Northeast, the numerous Vanderbilt progeny put their architectural stamp on other regions of the country. Most remarkable is Biltmore, George Washington Vanderbilt's ambitious estate near Asheville, North Carolina. Conceived as an entirely self-sufficient property, at 250 rooms it is believed to be the largest privately owned home in the United States. Everything from fruits, vegetables, wine, dairy products, and grains to lumber, honey from beehives, and wild game was among the bounty of Biltmore's 125,000 acres when it opened in 1895. Once again, Hunt was engaged as the architect. Frederick Law Olmsted, designer of Central Park in New York City and the Capitol grounds in Washington, D.C., did the landscaping.

Unlike the mansions of Newport, the North Carolina retreat was very much informed by a male sensibility. An area called the "Bachelor's Wing" was set off from the first floor through a doorway from the banquet hall and had a separate entrance through a *porte cochere* from the stable courtyard. The wing comprised a smoking room, with library, and a gun room, and was adjacent to a billiards room where ladies were welcome. Above the wing were rooms for unattached male guests, who could move easily from their chambers to the men's enclave.

In some ways, life at Biltmore resembled life in a grand hotel. The banquet hall sat 64 and the house could receive at least 30 overnight visitors quite comfortably. Of course, this meant employing a staff of some 50 people to serve the guests in high style. Vanderbilt, who had ties to the Teddy Roosevelt White House, included many politicians among his guests, so it is quite conceivable that high-level decisions were being made over cigars and brandy there.

The likely routine was for the gentlemen to retire to the smoking room until quite late at night, after the ladies had retired. However, the Victorian boundaries between ladies and smoking had broken down somewhat by the end of the century, and it was done by upper-class women—although it's not clear whether they smoked cigars or the newfangled cigarettes that had recently begun to be produced in the area.

The tycoon Henry Flagler's Palm Beach estate, Whitehall, below, was built as a wedding present for his wife. Although most of the home was decorated with her feminine touch, Flagler built himself a large billiard room, right, that doubled as his cigar retreat.

Like Ruggles Morse, Henry Flagler went from building hotels to outfitting his own house in grand style, but in his case it was done with much more wherewithal. Flagler made his original fortune as a partner of John D. Rockefeller in Standard Oil, and later almost single-handedly opened up Florida as a tourist mecca. Along the way he built railroads to carry travelers all the way to Key West and erected the hotels in which they would stay. In 1902, he finished his own accommodations—Whitehall, in Palm Beach—and gave the house as a wedding present to his wife, Mary Lily Kenan.

Designed by Carrére and Hastings, architect of the New York Public Library and the U.S. Senate and House of Representative

office buildings, it is a Beaux Arts masterpiece and undoubtedly the state's grandest residence. It would turn Palm Beach into the society enclave that it is today.

It is evident from the decor of most of the building, with its French salon and Louis XVI stylings, that his wife's feminine touch held great sway, but once again the billiard room became a place for men to gather. There Flagler had installed not one, but three tables: one for three-cushion billiards, one for pocket pool, and one for skittles. There is a large Caen stone fireplace, paintings applied directly to the walls, and a much darker color scheme overall than in the rest of the house. An Italian Renaissance library was apparently his domain as well.

The tycoon may have had to stand his ground to retain those two enclaves. In a letter to one of his interior designers, W.P. Stymus, he wrote: "It has just occurred to me that I haven't a cuspadore [sic] for Whitehall. I wish you would order for me one for each of the offices, two for the billiard room, and one for the library. Mrs. Flagler says she doesn't want one any elsewhere in the house."

Flagler's cigar retreat was passed on to a niece, who sold it. The investors turned the estate into a hotel that operated until 1959, when the building was recovered as a museum. As the Gilded Age ran its course, most of the grander homes would suffer similar fates as income tax, inheritance tax, and the cost of maintaining servant staffs had their considerable impact. In fact, Henry James coined the term "white elephant" to describe just such unmaintainable jewels. Newport, which once had 50 comparable mansions, now has just a half-dozen that are kept as residences. We can only take solace that some remain as museums where one can gaze upon the rooms where men once went to smoke fine cigars in a style that will probably never be enjoyed again.
                                                                    —JACK BETTRIDGE

Club Macanudo is one of New York City's premier cigar nightspots. With its opulent, majestic decor, Club Mac was the brainchild of Edgar M. Cullman Jr., chief executive officer of Culbro Corp. (General Cigar Company's parent company), who sought to create a haven for cigar-lovers ". . . where everything else is secondary."

Chapter

Friendly Atmospheres: Cigar Bars and More

Twelve

Come in here, dear boy. Have a cigar.

You're gonna go far. You're gonna fly high,

You're never gonna die. You're gonna

make it if you try. They're gonna love you.

—Pink Floyd, 1974

In what passes for the beginning of cigar culture,

Rodrigo de Xeres, who landed on the shores of Cuba with Christopher Columbus in 1492 looking for gold, "discovered" the cigar instead. And he saw that it was good.

Unreliable reports suggest that de Xeres then tried to open a cigar bar. Since few people in the 15th century had ever heard of, much less smoked, a cigar, no bank would give him a loan. Poor Rodrigo was born way ahead of his time. Today, the cigar bar seems an almost indispensable part of modern life.

While the cigar has long been seen as an ostentatious trapping of success

The exclusive Grand Havana Room in Beverly Hills, left, is considered by many to be the quintessential cigar-dedicated establishment. A favorite of such cigar-smoking Hollywood royalty as Mel Gibson and Gregory Hines, Grand Havana offers its members a haven in which to relax, have a drink, and light up a cigar. Grand Havana's New York location is particularly impressive, with its spectacular view from atop 666 Fifth Avenue, and its 800-locker humidor.

119

The success of Club Macanudo
in New York City led the
owners to open the popular
Punch Bar, located at
the Sheraton Hotel in the
Heart of Boston.
Frequented by both sea-
soned cigar aficionados
and by those seeking to
explore the hot new cigar
smoking trend, Punch
offers its guests a lively,
comfortable place to sit
back and enjoy a good
cigar.

120

smoked by show-offs, the bar dedicated to cigar smoking didn't really need to exist until recently. The restrictions on smoking just two decades ago were neither prevalent nor strict. Cigars might not have been allowed in restaurant smoking sections, but bars generally were accommodating.

Today, though, a squeaky-wheel segment of the "fun police" has declared that anything which is harmful if pursued in excess is wholly unacceptable, in moderation. The cigar boom and the collateral explosion in cigar bars are a reaction to the constant alarms of danger in pleasure. In addition, cigar bars are among the most stylish places at which one can smoke his or her own social statement.

These days, just calling your establishment a cigar bar is not enough. Yours is either "cigar dedicated"—where a good selection of cigars is sold, where the menu is designed to complement cigars, and where a special effort has been made to ventilate the environment; or "cigar friendly"—where you are at least allowed to smoke a cigar somewhere comfortable on the premises.

Perhaps today's quintessential "cigar-dedicated" establishment is the Grand Havana Room in Beverly Hills. (As this book goes to print, there are three Grand Havanas, with plans for more.) When the Beverly Hills flagship cigar bar was being imagined by Harry and Stan Shuster, along with actor Joe Pantoliano (whom the Shusters met through a mutual friend), the smart move was to make sure that the place was exclusive. In 1994, Grand Havana opened as a private club. Pantoliano—whose love of cigars had led to friendships with prominent people in the cigar industry, and who also knew everybody who was anybody among Hollywood's notable cigar aficionados—spearheaded the effort to recruit stars as charter members. Arnold

Schwarzenegger, Mel Gibson, and Jack Nicholson were all given lockers in a floor-to-ceiling humidor built into the concave wall of the previously unused second floor of an Italian restaurant. Others were charged $2,000, plus a $150 monthly rental fee, for a locker and a key to the elevator. The combination of stars and cigars told prospective members that this was going to be a special destination.

Grand Havana instantly became the darling of the cigar media and the humidor-away-from-home of industry insiders visiting L.A. The opening was featured in cigar publications as well as mainstream magazines, with photos of the cigar makers hanging out with the brightest lights in Tinseltown. What better impetus could there be for propelling a phenomenon?

On a given Saturday, if you happen by, you might bump into actor Joe Mantegna having lunch or smoking a cigar in the company of fellow thespian Chi McBride. A little later, Mel Gibson might walk in and talk movies over lunch and coronas on one of the club's two outdoor terraces. On a given Tuesday night during the baseball playoffs, you might have Gregory Hines sitting in front of you, eating dinner and jumping up whenever the Yankees did something good. The scene is more relaxed than might be expected in a Beverly Hills nightspot. There is no need to play big-shot by pulling a Cuban cigar out of your locker. Everybody has Cuban cigars in their locker if they want them.

"These cigar bars now draw a much younger group, the new wave of younger smokers. Grand Havana is geared more to the guy that's been smoking a long, long time and his passion is cigars," says Stan Shuster, Grand Havana's executive vice president. "A lot of these cigar bars now are a place to hang out, a place to meet a girl, a place to have a drink. . . . Mine's not that. Mine is more conducive to relaxing and smoking a cigar and having a nice drink. We're a private club, so a lot

Right: Located in New York City's fashionable Gramercy Park district, Cafe Aubette is a chic relaxing place to settle in and enjoy a drink and a cigar. Smokers should head past the bar and toward the plush leather couches in the back, where a small cabinet full of cigar boxes casts a cigar-friendly ambiance. Opposite: Located in Las Vegas' mega hotel, "New York, New York", Hamilton's—owned by the actor George Hamilton—is an elegant cigar-smoking establishment.

of these people who enjoy cigars can enjoy them in a situation where they know they're not going to be bothered."

Prominent at each of the Grand Havana Rooms is the humidor. The humidor in Washington holds 500 lockers. In New York, where anybody would be impressed just by the view from the top of 666 Fifth Avenue, there are 800 lockers in the humidor. In Beverly Hills, the 340 lockers are less imposing, but seem to fit as if the room had been built around them. The ceiling in Beverly Hills is round, and is painted in alternating slices of dark green and cigar-brown. It is complemented by a column that is painted to look like a cigar wrapper leaf, veins and all. That's about as strong a dedication to cigars as you are likely to find. Unless, of course, you happen to be on East 63rd Street in Manhattan.

Just off Madison Avenue is where you'll find the steps leading up to Club Macanudo, which was opened to the public in 1996 and is owned by General Cigar Company (the Connecticut-based manufacturer of Macanudo, Partagas and other fine brands). Club Macanudo sprang from the mind of top man Edgar M. Cullman Jr., chief executive officer of Culbro Corp. (General's parent company), who strived to create "a place for cigars, where everything else is secondary." The venture set the pace for New York's cigar rooms.

On any given night Club Mac might be so crowded that you'll have to wait behind the rope. The whole place holds only 125 people. Get past the antique cigar-store Indians and you might find Tom Selleck and Wilford Brimley having a drink and a smoke in the Bar Room, as members of the cigar nomenclature perch on the overstuffed sofas and club chairs. The guests sip mineral water, munch pizza (the menu

is limited to "snacks" because of New York's laws restricting smoking in full-service restaurants), and finish with a double espresso, all the while popping open one of the 500 rented lockers to fetch a super-premium robusto or Churchill. All around you there are reminders of the corporate connection: the matchboxes retain much of the design of the Macanudo cigar box, cigar art abounds, and merchandise like Partagas jackets occupy showcases near the entrance. Oh, and cigars from General are featured.

The building used to house a fairly opulent Italian restaurant and has retained some of its architectural finery. The ceiling in the Bar Room has red, green, and brown inlays, and the look of burlwood. The bar has a bronze top; the walls are embossed with tobacco leaves. The back third is the Club Room, where leaded windows filter the light and give the room a soft atmosphere.

Edgar Cullman's concept has been so successful that the Sheraton Hotel in Boston's Prudential Center has opened a cousin to Club Macanudo called the Punch Bar. It offers the hotel's guests a safe, comfortable place to have a cigar, and reaches out to Boston's permanent residents, as well. According to Punch's management, most of the patrons that frequent the establishment are local cigar aficionados, but about 25 percent of the guests are people who have never smoked a cigar and are looking to explore this hot

Baltimore's Havana Club was created for the many patrons of Ruth's Chris Steak House, who previously—due to smoking laws in Maryland—were unable to enjoy a fine cigar after dinner.

new trend. The management plans to multiply the Punch Bar in corporate-owned hotels everywhere.

Sporting a decor that could be characterized as "comfortably whimsical," the Punch Bar features a statue of Mr. Punch, for whom the bar is named. (While the cigar store Indian was a symbol for tobacco in North America, Mr. Punch was the symbol for tobacco and cigars in London.) The room also holds old copies of the defunct satirical British magazine Punch.

Maybe the best way of describing Butler's—the cigar bar in the Washington, D.C. Grand Hyatt—is "blue." Not blue as in "sad," but cobalt blue as in "cool." Butler's is open until two in the morning; soft jazz is piped into the dimly lit room where reproductions of Art Deco paintings inhabit the walls. The food, drink, and cigar menus are contained in cigar boxes on specially designed file cards. The fabric on the elegant, plush furniture is made of an unusually tight weave that helps prevent the smoke from penetrating and leaving an odor. Like any cigar-dedicated room worth frequenting, Butler's boasts an air-filtration system so you can enjoy your own cigar instead of the hodgepodge of smoke produced by everyone else's.

When the Grand Hyatt was considering remodeling its former lounge, the hotel's upscale clientele let it be known that they wanted something a bit more intimate than a hotel bar. In creating Butler's, the Grand Hyatt provided not only a sorely needed cigar room for an underserved part of the nation's capital, but also the prototype for sister hotels in search of a concept to increase revenues. Butler's has more than tripled the revenues of its predecessor in the same space.

Just a few blocks west of Butler's is Shelly's Back Room, a relatively casual room with lots of wood. The Back Room concept began as an adjunct to the full-size Shelly's Woodroast restaurant in suburban Maryland. The design reflects the company's "north woods" roots (the Back Room is owned by Minneapolis-based Woodroast Systems) and so does the menu.

Another unique aspect of Shelly's Back Room is its lack of pretension. As long as you're clothed and clean, you're welcome in the Back Room; it's known as a place where the owner of a gas station can meet the elite of Washington. And the cigars sold at Shelly's are some of the world's finest. This dedication to cigars is easy to understand, since Sheldon Jacobs (chairman and CEO of Woodroast Systems, Inc.) is one of the globe's preeminent collectors of Cuban cigars.

Shelly's Back Room is a place which many who work in the National Press Building across the street might visit every day for lunch and a torpedo. During the day, the room is definitely geared toward people with jobs; at night, the pace is a bit more leisurely. The Washington celebrities who are patrons prove that politics makes strange bedfellows—or maybe it's a common love of fine cigars which allows ideological opposites to share a table.

In a very accessible way, places like Shelly's Back Room are designed so that you can eat before you smoke a cigar. Nine other cities are scheduled to have a Shelly's at their service, but if you live and work in New York City, a very suitable substitute is Café Aubette. Aubette's cigar room is in the back. The front part of Aubette is a fairly typical, though prettier, version of a light-lunch gourmet coffee place. Past the bar you see the leather sofa and chairs across from a small cabinet full of cigar boxes. That should make it clear that your cutter is welcome to slice the business end off your favorite cigar.

Back in Washington, D.C., you can easily find a great steak at any number of restaurants, but at Sam & Harry's you'll also find a recently added and remodeled smoking area in the front of the restaurant adjacent to the bar. This appealing room is visible from the street.

Sam & Harry's fits the mold of many steakhouses—comfortable, with cases of wine sharing space with tables. The decor includes original paintings and sculptures based on blues and jazz. If you forget your cigars, don't worry; Sam & Harry's has an excellent variety stored in its J.C. Pendergast cabinet humidor, and the prices are reasonable. This is one of a growing number of restaurants where the owners—cigar smokers Larry Work and Michael Sternberg have seen the wisdom of encouraging aficionados to stay on after their meal to enjoy their double coronas at the same table. Ideally, the patron will also have an after-dinner beverage. That makes Sam & Harry's more enjoyable, and more profitable.

People were staying on after dinner at Baltimore's Ruth's Chris Steak House, but there was too little space in the bar area. Maryland law calls for a separate room in which smokers could also dine, but there was no room inside the first floor restaurant, so Cuban-born owner Steve de Castro remodeled his building's third floor. A blackboard in the small elevator lists the day's high and low temperatures—in Havana. When the door opens to let you out, you step into what was initially contemplated as a dessert room where diners could go after devouring "serious" steaks downstairs. Instead, it's now a cigar lounge called—what else?—the Havana Club. Dessert is still available, but you can also shoot pool, watch TV, have a drink, or just chat with your friends. On Friday and Saturday nights, people wait up to two hours to get in so they can dance to the live sounds of Latin and swing under a revolving mirrored globe. Other nights, it's easier to appreciate that this is a serious cigar place.

When the Havana Club opened, the cigar lockers immediately sold out and they had to build more. There are now 210 lockers along the walls, with leather chairs and other furniture. Sofas break up the room into smaller dens, and there's not too much dark wood. A tan ceiling lightens up the room, as do the lamps, which evoke the feel of Old Havana or the Latin Quarter of New Orleans.

Take a northbound train for about 90 minutes and you can enjoy a

Shelly's Back Room at Shelly's Woodroast restaurant in Rockville, Maryland (and Washington, D.C.) was designed for cigar lovers who want a place to kick back their feet, relax and sip Scotch or Cognac.

In Philadelphia, Holt's Cigar Co.—a retail tobacco store that provides its patrons with a fabulous smoking lounge—is considered an institution.

Philadelphia landmark: the Holt Cigar Co. on Walnut Street. Sure, it's a great cigar store, but Holt's has something more. . . . In the back of the store is a smoking lounge where you can sit in blue chairs and smoke your recent purchase. Holt's is not a cigar bar, but like one, it provides a sanctuary from the day's demons.

"Obviously, we want you to buy our cigars," said Robert Levin, owner of Holt's and the Ashton label, "but even more important is that you enjoy them. If we can help you do that, especially in the middle of a busy day, we are happy to do that extra little bit."

Going the extra mile is what Shareef Malnik did when he completely refashioned his successful Cuba Club—part of his venerable Forge restaurant—in very cigar-friendly Miami Beach. In a region which depends heavily on tourists from Europe, Malnik joined with Regine Choukroun in the fall of 1997 to create JIMMY'Z at Cuba Club. So now, on 41st Street, otherwise known as Arthur Godfrey Boulevard, European DJ's will keep you dancing, the "Blue Velvet Bar" will provide fine spirits, and the sunken living room known as "The Trophy Bedroom" will spur your fantasies. This private cigar spot retained its "Fuente Fuente Opus X" walk-in humidor, where stars like Sylvester Stallone, Madonna, and Matt Dillon hold private "vaults."

Perhaps the highlight of JIMMY'Z at Cuba Club is the "Champagne Caviar Room," cleverly named for the comestibles served there. The walls are "luxurious red," and the surrounding chairs and banquettes are "crushed tomato and gold." There are plenty of big mirrors for the rich and famous to make sure they look marvelous by the light of the opulent chandelier.

"We believe in ourselves, we adapt to change, and we keep everything fresh: from our business philosophy to every ingredient in our recipes," Malnik explained. "I'm convinced we've done well because we haven't lost focus on what our patron wants."

It's that focus which makes regulars out of customers—an idea that Jack Schwartz Importers in Chicago understands as well. In its humidor are a bench and one chair; next to the chair is a parking meter. For a quarter, you get ten minutes in the chair. After that, someone else gets a turn, so you might wander one block south in the Loop's financial district to the building which holds the Chicago Board of Options Exchange. There you'll find the entrance to the LaSalle Club, a state-of-the-art fitness center and 19-room hotel. The LaSalle Club is private, but many of the members work in the financial industry. If you can hook up with one of them, or get one of the charming fellows at Jack Schwartz's to make a call for you, you might be able to sit in the Buckingham Grill and puff away while eavesdropping on conversations about the performance of the various markets that day. Pretend not to listen while you gaze through the arched window facing Congress Street at Chicago commuters.

The Buckingham Grill embodies the raw energy of capitalism. Traders having a single-malt Scotch with their cigar are likely to have just worked out for an hour—the epitome of the "work hard, play hard" gestalt. The grill is not a large space, but it is a very comfortable and true representation of the "broad shoulder" reputation of this city.

If the LaSalle Club remains inaccessible, two other Chicago hotels can provide luxurious service and surroundings for the cigar smoker in you. Everyone knows the Four Seasons is wonderful, but a bit farther south on Michigan Avenue is the Intercontinental Hotel's Bar Salon, a favorite of many of the staff at the neighboring *Chicago Tribune*. This piano bar is a great place to smoke and listen and thaw out. The room is dark and the sofas are overstuffed. Drinks come quickly and are ample, but you should take your own cigars, as the few for sale in the hotel's gift shop are expensive.

In Las Vegas, actor George Hamilton has taken a bit of New York's Rainbow Room (with faux windows framing photos of the Manhattan skyline) and added touches from old celebrity haunts like El Morocco and the Stork Club to create an elegant getaway from the frenetic pace of the casinos. Located in the New York, New York mega-hotel,

Hamilton's is also a cigar bar with a sense of humor. A display case outside the entrance shows off photos of George Hamilton escorting Elizabeth Taylor (who is popping out of her dress), George Hamilton escorting Joan Collins (who is popping out of her dress), and George Hamilton with Elvis. The main room has a leopard-print carpet. A private "Club Car" recreates the feel of an old train ride, complete with red velour banquettes and a one-way window looking out on the casino floor. No detail is overlooked. Even the matchsticks complement the decor, with a red phosphorous tip atop a black stick. While Hamilton's is part of the hotel, it also manages to maintain its own identity, achieving a special magic in a city where smoking is allowed everywhere.

In contrast to Vegas, the northwestern United States is plagued by legal restrictions on cigar smoking—and by high prices as well. The area from San Francisco to Seattle boasts some of the best restaurants and scenery around, but to fully enjoy a cigar experience here, plan ahead and plan on spending some major cash if you are traveling without a well-stocked humidor.

A recent trip to San Francisco left a visiting conference speaker with a dilemma: A major sporting event on the East Coast was available only via satellite on the TV in the hotel bar. Upon arriving at the bar and ordering a beer, then unsheathing a long-awaited double corona, the speaker heard the dreaded words, "I'm sorry, sir. No smoking allowed." What to do? In this case, the cigar waited. Next time? Pick the right hotel. In San Francisco, you won't be able to do much better than Nob Hill's Renaissance Stanford Court Hotel, named after railroad baron Leland Stanford (as in Stanford University), who originally built his mansion here in 1876. Expect great rooms, a great restaurant, and great service. But more pertinent to this discussion is the fact that the Stanford Court's management, led by Christopher Steuri, has responded to many guests by making fully half of its elegant lobby lounge a smoking area, adhering to the law by forsaking food service there.

Walk across the Oriental carpets and Carrarra marble to the other side if you want to eat, then walk back and light up. Look up to admire the Tiffany-style glass dome above the lobby as well as the nineteenth-century Baccarat chandeliers. The one above the staircase leading down to the ballrooms is from the Rothschild residence in France. Some of the mirrors are eighteenth-century originals bought at auction from the Grand Hotel in Paris. All these and other objects are within view of the cigar area of the bar.

As in most cities, there are a number of attractive alternatives available in San Francisco if you want to leave the hotel just to smoke a cigar somewhere other than your room. Among the most user-friendly is Fume, a mere two blocks from another "must" in San Francisco, the largest Nordstrom department store in the country. There's a Japanese restaurant on top of this narrow, sparsely decorated bar, which opens in mid-afternoon. There's not much of a crowd then, as most locals are still at work. Snag a table and smoke in peace.

If you travel northwards into Oregon, you'll be hit with a 65 percent tax on any tobacco product you purchase. Don't. Don't buy in the state of Washington, either, where the tax is 75 percent, the highest in the nation. If Seattle is your destination, you'll be glad you didn't spend money on cigars so that you can better afford dining at El Gaucho, with its dramatic midnight-blue walls. Before dinner, be sure to inform the staff you would like to go to the cigar room for the fruit, nut, and

Located on Miami's South Beach, JIMMY'Z at Cuba Club was created in celebration of everything Cuban. With its "Champagne Caviar Room," "Blue Velvet Bar," and sunken living room known as "The Trophy Bedroom," the club offers unparalleled excitement and opulence. Stars such as Sylvester Stallone, Madonna, and Matt Dillon each hold private "vaults" in the club's magnificent "Fuente Fuente Opus X" walk-in humidor.

staffers know you're spending big and they want to make sure you're getting your money's worth.

cheese course, dessert, and coffee. That will reserve you a space in one of the most desirable places to be seen lighting up a cigar.

El Gaucho's cigar lounge is casual or elegant, depending on how you want to dress that night, but it is always comfortable. The most attractive aspect of the entire restaurant, and especially the cigar room, is the attention to detail provided by tuxedoed servers. El Gaucho, like any good cigar place, is dedicated to your pleasure. The

Every cigar bar in every city across the country offers something special. Ultimately, the people who work at your favorite spot are the ones who make you feel welcome there. The point is to find a cigar room you like and in which you feel comfortable. If you travel a lot, you will always have a welcome challenge—finding a good place to smoke your favorite cigar. If you don't travel, no doubt you have already found the place where everybody knows your name. —ALEJANDRO BENES

131

Photography Credits

p. 2: Jeff Harris

p. 6, 7: Clockwise from top center: Jeff Harris; Courtesy of the Grand Havana Room; Gene Coleman; Roger Jacobs.

p. 8: Brad Trent

p. 10: Roger Jacobs

pp. 13, 14: Jeff Harris

p. 15: Courtesy of Kreitman-Thelen

p. 16: Jonathan L. Smith

p. 17: Jeff Harris

pp. 18, 19, 20: Jonathan L. Smith

pp. 21, 22: Jeff Harris

p. 25: Courtesy of the Boston Cigar Co.

pp. 26, 28, 29: Jeff Harris

p. 30: Courtesy of Davidoff

pp. 32, 34, 36, 38: From the Collection of Howard J. Thomas/Photos by Walter P. Calahan

pp. 42, 45, 46, 49, 51, 52, 54: Jeff Harris

p. 56, 57: Courtesy of the National Lighter Museum

p. 59: Courtesy of Cartier

pp. 60, 63, 65: Jeff Harris

p. 66: Jonathan L. Smith

pp. 68, 69: Jeff Harris

pp. 70, 72, 74: Gene Coleman

p. 76: Jeff Harris

pp. 77, 78: Gene Coleman

p. 80: Jody Erdman

p. 83: Clifford A. Wollach

pp. 85, 86, 87: Jody Erdman

p. 88: John Harding

p. 91: John Harding; "The Bruiser" by John Grossman

p. 92, 93: John Harding

p. 94, 96: Courtney Grant Winston

p. 99: Corbis-Bettmann

p. 100: Figures from the Museum of American Folk Art/ Photos by Brooks Kraft/Sygma

p. 102: Courtesy of The Preservation Society of Newport County

p. 105: Courtesy of The Biltmore Company

pp. 106, 107: Courtesy of The Preservation Society of Newport County

pp. 108, 109: Tim Fields

pp. 110, 111: The Biltmore Company

pp. 114, 115: Henry M. Flagler

p. 116: Courtesy of Club Macanudo

p. 119: Courtesy of Grand Havana Room

p. 120: Courtesy of Punch Bar

p. 122: Courtesy of Cafe Aubette

p. 123: David Glomb

p. 124: Courtesy of the Havana Club

p. 127: Courtesy of Shelly's Woodroast Restaurant & Shelly's Back Room

p. 128: Courtesy of Holt's Cigar Co.

p. 131: Gaston Pacheco/Courtesy of Jimmy'z at Cuba Club